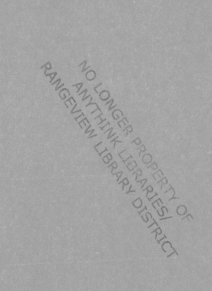

Surprise *Cakes*

35 delicious cakes to delight and amaze

Race Point
PUBLISHING

Marsha Phipps

Race Point Publishing
A division of Quarto Publishing Group USA Inc.
276 Fifth Avenue, Suite 205
New York, NY 10001

RACE POINT and the distinctive Race Point Publishing logo are
trademarks of Quarto Publishing Group USA Inc.

This 2015 edition published by Race Point Publishing by arrangement with
Quintet Publishing Limited.

This book was conceived, designed, and produced by:
Quintet Publishing Limited
4th Floor, Sheridan House
114–116 Western Road
Hove, East Sussex BN3 1DD
United Kingdom

Project Editor: Salima Hirani
Designer: Geoff Borin
Photographer: Tony Briscoe
Art Director: Michael Charles
Editorial Assistant: Ella Lines
Publishing Assistant: Alice Sambrook
Editorial Director: Emma Bastow
Publisher: Mark Searle

Library of Congress Cataloging-in-Publication data is available

ISBN-13: 978-1-631060-34-2

Printed and bound in China By RR Donnelley

2 4 6 8 10 9 7 5 3 1

www.racepointpub.com

Contents

Introduction

A spectacular cake always boosts a party, whether it's a wedding, a child's birthday party, or any special gathering to celebrate an important event. And people are always happy to see cake—it's a fact! So imagine their delight when the gorgeous, tempting cake is finally cut open to reveal something unexpected on the inside!

It's very gratifying to see a little girl's eyes light up when her birthday cake is cut open and bonbons tumble out, or someone's thrill as they see their name proudly billboarded on a delicious slice of cake that's presented to them. Surprise cakes are fun to make and delightful to receive and share. They are also fun to design. I have spent years baking cakes for all sorts of events, and my clients have provided many opportunities for me to design and create cakes with a hidden surprise that brings in another level of enjoyment, once the cake is cut and the surprise is revealed.

As a self-taught baker and cake decorator, I can tell you that making spectacular cakes is very achievable, even for a novice baker. In this book I share the techniques I use to give my cakes a 'wow' factor, along with some of the recipes I use to make delicious cakes of different flavors. In the individual cake projects, I pair the recipes with decorating techniques to provide cake designs that you can recreate for your own special events. All the cake projects are adaptable, so once you are comfortable with the techniques, you'll be able to mix and match your new skills to create any number of variations on the cake designs. With this book to guide you,

you'll learn how to make dazzling cakes that will delight your family and friends.

Before you reach for your apron, read through the techniques given at the beginning of the book. These are referred to within the cake projects, along with the basic recipes used to make many of the cake projects in this book. Read the entire recipe and method for making up a cake design before you begin working on it, and ensure you have all of your ingredients and tools to hand. Also, observe the preparation times provided with each project. Some projects require you to make certain preparations the night before, such as preparing a cake presentation board, making ganache, or pre-baking specific items. At the back of the book I provide templates used to make some of the cake projects. These can be photocopied and cut out, and the cake projects will guide you on how to use them.

I hope that you enjoy making the projects in this book. Once you've mastered the basic skills, perhaps my ideas will inspire you to dream up some fantastic designs to surprise the lucky recipients of your creations!

Marsha Phipps

Tools

With a little flair and ingenuity, you can create cute and pretty cakes, but with the right tools, you can turn out some spectacular confections that look professionally made. If you bake regularly, it's worth investing in a few of these items. Below is a list of tools I couldn't do without. None of them are particularly expensive, and all of them make the job of producing a show-stopping surprise cake that much more achievable.

Cake boards

Cake presentation boards are used for many of the projects in this book because they help to showcase the cake design. Each project states the diameter of the cake board required. Opt for boards that are about ½ inch (12 mm) thick. These can be covered with a ⅛-inch (3-mm) thick covering of fondant. The edge of the board can be wrapped with a ⅝-inch (15-mm) wide ribbon.

Cake leveler

This tool is easy to use (see page 18) and great for cutting off uneven cake tops, leaving you with perfectly flat cake layers that will stack comfortably and neatly.

Cake plate

A cake plate is an elegant accessory for showcasing your creations and can be used in place of a presentation board.

Cake-release spray

For cases in which parchment paper liners cannot be used, cake release spray is great. Use it with dome-shaped shaped cake pans and cake pop molds.

Cake smoothers

These allow you to create a smooth, bump-free surface when covering a cake or board in fondant.

Cake tester

This handy tool helps you to check whether or not your cake is baked.

Cake pans

A good-quality set of cake pans can help you to produce well-baked cakes. Buy the heavy-duty kind for longevity. For the projects in this book, you'll need the following bakeware:

• 8-inch (20-cm) round sandwich cake pans—you'll need a maximum of four for multiple cake layers, so you can bake them simultaneously, but you can make do with fewer pans and bake in batches

- round cake pans in two sizes: a 6-inch (15-cm) pan and an 8-inch (20-cm) pan
- an 8-inch (20-cm) square cake pan
- a dome-shaped cake pan or a heatproof glass bowl with a diameter of 6 inches (15 cm)
- a 2 lb (900 g) loaf pan
- a silicone 12-hole cupcake pan
- a cake pop mold with 12 cake pop recesses
- a cookie sheet and baking sheet.

Cooling rack

A good-quality high cooling rack will allow your cakes to cool thoroughly and quickly.

Cupcake liners

These are available in a wide range of colors and patterns for adding an extra pop of color to your parties. You can use either paper liners set in a 12-hole cupcake pan, or a silicone 12-hole cupcake pan, which should be set on a baking sheet.

Cookie/pastry cutters

Cutters of all shapes and sizes are available online. In this book, I use flower-shaped cutters, a star-shaped cutter, round cutters, and letter-shapes.

Disposable pastry bags

These are cheap to easy to use (see page 24). Use them to apply frostings to cakes and for adding batter to a cake pan without disturbing frozen cake shapes you've positioned in the pan.

Dough scrapers

Dough scrapers help you to create perfectly smooth layers of buttercream and ganache on your cakes.

Edible paint and glitter

Add some flair to your designs with these edible decorative applications.

Fondant

A good-quality fondant has a balance of elasticity and softness and tastes great with your cakes. Roll out fondant on a surface dusted with confectioner's sugar. Save extra fondant by storing it in a resealable food bag to keep it soft. Wrap up any fondant you're not working on in plastic wrap to keep it soft.

Gel food colors

These give your cakes and frostings a vibrancy of color that you cannot achieve with liquid colorings. Use a toothpick to add small amounts to cake batter or frosting and add more until you achieve the shade and brightness you desire.

Ice cream scoop

An ice cream scoop with a spring-release button is ideal for portioning out cupcake batter.

Knives

Paring knives are great for making small, precise cuts when shaping cakes, and a long serrated cake knife can slice through a cake with ease.

Gumpaste

This is firmer and more pliable than fondant and can be rolled out more thinly, so is great for forming sugar decorations for your cakes. Roll out gumpaste on a surface dusted with confectioner's sugar.

Nonstick rolling pins

These are ideal for rolling out fondant and gumpaste. It's useful to have both a large (8-inch/20-cm) and a small (4-inch/10-cm) nonstick rolling pin.

Paintbrush

A paintbrush, used only for baking projects, is the perfect tool for applying a little water to gumpaste decorations in order to stick them onto cakes.

Piping tips

If you like to bake cakes and cupcakes, you may already have a good range of piping tips. For the projects in this book, I mostly use a cupcake filling tip (Wilton 230) and a star piping tip (Wilton 1M).

Silicone spatula

Silicone spatulas are great for scraping every bit of batter out of your bowl. Once you've used one, you won't know how you ever coped without one!

Spatulas

A selection of spatulas in different sizes will help you to apply ganache or buttercream evenly to your cake surfaces. Angled metal spatulas are particularly useful, as the cranked handle gives you a good angle to work from when applying frostings.

Stand mixer

This piece of kit is expensive, but is so useful in the kitchen, it's well worth the investment if you like to cook. It makes mixing batter a much quicker and easier job. If you don't have a stand mixer, use a hand-held electric whisk or a hand blender instead.

Toothpicks

This simple, versatile tool is great for testing cakes, marking sections of cakes (so you know which is the front when you've baked a surprise into the center of your cake), and making gumpaste models.

Turntable

A turntable enables you to rotate a cake while decorating it. It is especially useful when applying a continuous decoration, such as a spiral, around the sides of a cake.

Basic Recipes

In this section I provide recipes for a variety of basic cakes, each with different batch sizes to help you make the size of cake needed for your particular project. I also share my favorite frosting recipes and provide a guide to help you flavor your cakes and frostings, so you can adapt the cake projects in this book to suit the occasion, the people you'll be sharing the cakes with, or your own tastes.

When you have reliable recipes to fall back on, baking delicious cakes becomes easy, so you can focus your efforts on the design and decoration of your masterpieces. I use the recipes given here in my work repeatedly, so they are my tried and tested favorites.

The projects in this book refer to these basic recipes, requiring pre-baked cakes of a specific size/shape, a batch of batter of a specific size, and/or a batch of frosting. In some cases, you may have some batter left over from making the cake. Either discard it, or use it to whip up a few cupcakes or another cake.

Flavoring cakes and frostings

Apart from the Chocolate Cake (see page 14) and the Swiss Meringue Buttercream (see page 16), the cakes and frostings in this section can be flavored using the quantities of flavorings suggested below.

Flavor	Cake (small or medium batch)	Cake (large batch)	Frosting
Vanilla	1 tsp vanilla essence	1 tsp vanilla essence	1tsp vanilla essence
Chocolate	1 tbsp unsweetened cocoa powder	2 tbsp unsweetened cocoa powder	2 tbsp unsweetened cocoa powder
Almond	1 tsp almond essence	2 tsp almond essence	1 tsp almond essence
Lemon	2 tbsp lemon juice plus the grated zest of ½ medium lemon	4 tbsp lemon juice plus the grated zest of 1 medium lemon	2 tbsp lemon juice plus the grated zest of 1 lemon
Orange	3 tbsp orange juice plus the grated zest of ½ medium orange	5 tbsp orange juice plus the grated zest of 1 medium orange	tbsp orange juice plus the grated zest of 1 orange

Classic Vanilla Cake

This recipe makes a versatile classic sponge cake that can be used for cakes, loafs, and cupcakes. It is strong enough to hold additional weight, so opt for this recipe if covering your cake with fondant or making cakes that are baked with shaped pieces of cake inside them.

Preparation time: 1–2 hours (depending on the size of pan used)

Large batch
• **1 cake baked in an 8-inch (20-cm) square or round cake pan (Servings: 15–20)**
•**1 loaf baked in a 2 lb (900 g) loaf pan (Servings: 10)**
• **3 cake layers baked in 3 × 8-inch (20-cm) sandwich cake pans (Servings: 8–10)**

2 cups (14 oz/400 g) superfine sugar
1⅔ cups (14 oz/400 g) unsalted butter, softened
3½ cups (14 oz/400 g) all-purpose flour
7 large eggs, at room temperature
1 tsp vanilla extract
Gel food coloring (optional)

Small batch
12 cupcakes (Servings: 12)

1 cup + 1 tbsp (5½ oz/150 g) unsalted butter, softened
¾ cup (5½ oz/150 g) superfine sugar
2 large eggs, at room temperature
1¼ cups + 2 tbsp (5½ oz/150 g) all-purpose flour
1 tsp vanilla extract
Gel food coloring (optional)

To make cakes

1. Preheat oven to 325ºF (160ºC). Line your cake pan(s) with parchment paper.

2. Set a stand mixer fitted with a paddle attachment to a medium speed and cream together the butter and sugar in the stand mixer bowl until the mixture is pale and fluffy. Using a silicone spatula, scrape down the sides of the bowl and mix again for 1 minute.

3. Add the eggs one at a time and continue to mix until they are incorporated. Scrape down the sides of the bowl once more and mix again for 1 minute.

4. Sift the flour into the mixture and continue to mix until it is incorporated.

5. Add the vanilla extract. If you are coloring the sponge, reduce the stand mixer's speed setting to slow and add small amounts of gel coloring at a time using a toothpick (allowing the mixer to blend the color for you) until you have the desired shade.

6. Now pour the batter into the prepared pan(s). Bake for 50 minutes to 1 hour and 10 minutes until a cake tester comes out clean. Leave to cool in the pan(s) for 10 minutes, then thurn out onto a wire rack and leave and leave to cool completely.

To make cupcakes

1. Preheat oven to 325ºF (160ºC). Set 12 cupcake liners in a 12-hole cupcake pan or a silicone 12-hole cupcake pan on a baking sheet. Follow steps 2–5 above to make the batter. Portion out the batter into the cupcake liners using an ice cream scoop (see page 24).

2. Bake for 20–25 minutes, until the sponge bounces back when gently tapped. Remove immediately from the cupcake pan or baking sheet and leave on a wire rack to cool.

Gluten-free Vanilla Cake

This tasty and reliable recipe can be used as a substitute for the Vanilla Cake (see page 11) if you're baking for anyone with a gluten allergy.

Preparation time: 1–2 hours (depending on the size of pan used)

Large batch
• **1 cake baked in an 8-inch (20-cm) square or round cake pan** **(Servings: 15–20)**
•**1 loaf baked in a 2 lb (900 g) loaf pan** **(Servings: 10)**
• **3 cake layers baked in 3 × 8-inch (20-cm) sandwich cake pans** **(Servings: 8–10)**

1⅔ cups (14 oz/400 g) unsalted butter, softened
2 cups (14 oz/400 g) superfine sugar
7 large eggs, at room temperature
8 tbsp whole milk
3½ cups (14 oz/400 g) gluten-free all-purpose flour
2 tsp baking powder
¼ tsp salt
2 tsp xanthan gum
5 tsp vanilla extract
Gel food color (optional)

Small batch
12 cupcakes (Servings: 12)

1 cup + 1 tbsp (5½ oz/150 g) unsalted butter, softened
¾ cup (5½ oz/150 g) superfine sugar
2 large eggs, at room temperature
3 tbsp whole milk
1¼ cups + 2 tbsp (5½ oz/150 g) gluten-free all-purpose flour

1 tsp baking powder
2 tsp vanilla extract
⅛ tsp salt
1 tsp xanthan gum
Gel food color (optional)

To make cakes

1. Preheat oven to 325ºF (160ºC). Line your cake pan(s) with parchment paper.

2. Set a stand mixer fitted with a paddle attachment to a medium speed. Cream together the butter and sugar until pale and fluffy. Using a silicone spatula, scrape down the sides of the bowl and mix again for 1 minute.

3. Add the eggs one at a time and continue to mix until incorporated. Scrape down the sides of the bowl and add the milk. Mix again for 1 minute.

4. Sift in the flour and baking powder. Add the salt and xanthan gum and mix until incorporated.

5. Mix in the vanilla extract (or another flavoring). If you are coloring the sponge, reduce the mixer's speed setting to slow and add small amounts at a time using a toothpick (allowing the mixer to blend the color for you) until you have the desired shade.

6. Pour the batter into the prepared pan(s) and bake for 50 minutes to 1 hour and 10 minutes until a cake tester comes out clean. Leave to cool in the pan(s) for 10 minutes, then turn out onto a wire rack and leave to cook completely.

To make cupcakes

Preheat oven to 325ºF (160ºC). Set 12 cupcake liners in a cupcake pan or a silicone pan on a baking sheet. Follow steps 2–5 above and portion out the batter into the liners. Bake for 20–25 minutes, until the sponge bounces back when gently tapped.

White Cake

This cake is the perfect starting point for making colored cakes as the batter takes on any color very effectively. This recipe produces a delicious soft white sponge. For flavor variations, add an extract (such as mint or rose) or the grated zest of lemon or orange.

Preparation time: 1–2 hours (depending on the size of pan used)

Large batch
3 cake layers baked in 3 × 8-inch (20-cm) sandwich cake pans (Servings: 8–10)

1 cup (8 oz/225 g) unsalted butter, softened
2¼ cups (1 lb/450 g) superfine sugar
3½ cups (14 oz/400 g) self-rising flour
2 pinches of salt
1 cup + 2 tbsp (9 fl oz/250 ml) whole milk
6 extra-large egg whites
Gel food coloring (optional)

Medium batch
• **1 cake baked in an 8-inch (20-cm) square or round cake pan (Servings: 15–20)**
• **1 loaf baked in a 2 lb (900 g) loaf pan (Servings: 10)**

¾ cup (6 oz/175 g) unsalted butter, softened
1½ cups (11¾ oz/340 g) superfine sugar
2½ cups + 2 tbsp (10½ oz/300 g) self-rising flour
Pinch of salt
¾ cup + 2 tbsp (7 fl oz/200 ml) whole milk
4 extra-large egg whites
Gel food coloring (optional)

Small batch
12 cupcakes (Servings: 12)

½ cup (4 oz/115 g) unsalted butter, softened
1 cup + 2 tbsp (8 oz/225 g) superfine sugar
1⅔ cups (7 oz/200 g) self-rising flour
Pinch of salt
½ cup (4 fl oz/125 ml) whole milk
3 extra-large egg whites
Gel food coloring (optional)

To make cakes

1. Preheat oven to 325ºF (160ºC). Line your cake pan(s) with parchment paper. Set a stand mixer fitted with a paddle attachment to a medium speed. Cream together the butter and sugar for at least 5 minutes. Scrape down the sides of the bowl and mix for 1 minute.

2. Meanwhile, sift the flour into a large bowl with the salt. Set aside.

3. Stir the milk and egg whites together gently.

4. Add half the flour to the creamed butter and sugar mixture and mix on a medium speed. Then add half of the milk and egg white mixture. Once combined, scrape down the sides of the bowl and repeat the process, adding the remaining flour first, then the remaining milk and egg white mixture.

5. Add a flavoring at this point, if using one. If you are coloring the sponge, reduce the mixer's speed setting to slow and add small amounts at a time using a toothpick (allowing the stand mixer to blend the color for you) until you have the desired shade.

6. Pour the batter into the prepared pan(s). Bake a medium batch for 30–40 minutes or a large batch for 55 minutes until a cake tester comes out clean. Leave to cool in the pan(s) for 10 minutes, then turn out onto a wire rack and leave to cool.

To make cupcakes

1. Preheat oven to 325ºF (160ºC). Set 12 cupcake liners in a 12-hole cupcake pan or a silicone 12-hole cupcake pan on a baking sheet. Follow steps 2–5 above to make the batter. Portion out the batter into the liners using an ice cream scoop.

2. Bake for 20–25 minutes, until the sponge springs back when gently tapped. Remove immediately from the cupcake pan or baking sheet and leave on a wire rack to cool.

Chocolate Cake

This divine cake is one of my personal favorites. It pairs a rich flavor with a light, fluffy texture to produce a sponge that is firm enough to cover withstand a covering of fondant.

Preparation time: 2 hours (depending on the size of pan used)

Large batch
3 cake layers baked in 3 × 8-inch (20-cm) sandwich cake pans (Servings: 8–10)
1 cup (7 oz/200 g) unsalted butter, softened
2½ cups (1 lb 2 oz/500 g) superfine sugar
4 large eggs, at room temperature
2 vanilla extract
1 cup (3½ oz/100 g) unsweetened cocoa powder
2 tsp baking powder
2 tsp baking soda
2 pinches of salt
3 cups (12 oz/350 g) all-purpose flour
1¼ cups + 2 tbsp (11 fl oz/325 ml) whole milk

Medium batch
• 1 cake baked in an 8-inch (20-cm) square or round cake pan (Servings: 15–20)
•1 loaf baked in a 2 lb (900 g) loaf pan (Servings: 10)
½ cup + 1 tbsp (5½ oz/150 g) unsalted butter, softened
1¾ cups (13 oz/375 g) superfine sugar
3 large eggs, at room temperature
1½ tsp vanilla extract
⅔ cup (2½ oz/70 g) unsweetened cocoa powder
1 tsp baking powder
1 tsp baking soda
Pinch of salt
2⅓ cups (9½ oz/265 g) all-purpose flour
1 cup (8½ fl oz/240 ml) whole milk

Small batch
12 cupcakes (Servings: 12)
½ cup (3½ oz/100 g) unsalted butter, softened
1 cup + 3 tbsp (9 oz/250 g) superfine sugar
2 large eggs, at room temperature
1 tsp vanilla extract
½ cup (1¾ oz/50 g) unsweetened cocoa powder
1 tsp baking powder

1 tsp baking soda
Pinch of salt
1½ cups (6 oz/175 g) all-purpose flour
⅔ cup + 1 tbsp (5½ fl oz/160 ml) whole milk

To make cakes

1. Preheat the oven to 325ºF (160ºC). Line your cake pan(s) with parchment paper.

2. Set a stand mixer with a paddle attachment to a medium speed. Cream together the butter and sugar until pale and fluffy. Scrape down the bowl and mix again for 1 minute. Add the eggs one at a time and mix until incorporated. Scrape down the sides of the bowl once more and mix again for 1 minute.

3. Set the mixer speed to slow. Mix in the vanilla, cocoa powder, baking powder, baking soda, and salt.

4. Sift half the flour into the batter, increase the speed to medium, then mix in half the milk. Scrape down the bowl, then sift in the remaining flour and add the remaining milk and mix until incorporated.

5. Pour the batter into the prepared pan(s). Bake a medium batch for 30–40 minutes or a large batch for 50 minutes until a cake tester comes out clean. Cool in pan(s) for 10 minutes, then turn out onto a wire rack and allow to cool.

To make cupcakes

1. Preheat oven to 325ºF (160ºC). Set 12 cupcake liners in a 12-hole cupcake pan or a silicone 12-hole cupcake pan on a baking sheet. Follow steps 2–3 above to make the batter. Portion out the batter into the liners using an ice cream scoop.

2. Bake for 20–25 minutes until the sponge springs back when tapped. Lleave on a wire rack to cool.

Basic Recipes

Classic Buttercream

Quick and simple and absolutely delicious, this buttercream continues to be a favorite frosting with bakers around the world. It is rich, sweet and firm, so it forms a nice base for fondant decoration, and is perfect for decorating cupcakes. This recipe can be easily adapted by choosing different flavors of extract, or cocoa powder for chocolate buttercream.

Preparation time: 10 minutes

Portion: Enough to fill and cover an 8-inch (20-cm) cake with 3 layers or top at least 12 cupcakes

3½ cups (1 lb 2 oz/500 g) confectioner's sugar
1 cup (9 oz/250 g) unsalted butter, softened
    and cubed
1 tbsp milk
1 tsp vanilla extract
Gel food color (optional)

1. Pour the confectioner's sugar into the bowl of a stand mixer fitted with a paddle attachment and set to medium speed. One by one, add the cubes of butter and allow them to be slowly mixed into the sugar. It may take a minute or two for the buttercream to begin to form, so be patient.

2. Once all the butter is incorporated, add the milk and continue to mix on a medium speed. Once the milk is incorporated, leave the mixer to continue blending the mixture on a high speed for about 5 minutes until the frosting is light and fluffy.

3. Add the vanilla extract (or another flavoring of your choice). If you are coloring the frosting, use gel food color. Reduce the stand mixer's speed setting to slow and add small amounts at a time using a toothpick (allowing the stand mixer to blend the color for you) until you have the desired shade.

Swiss Meringue Buttercream

Making Swiss Meringue Buttercream can be a little more labour intensive than your traditional buttercream, but once you have tasted it you'll know it is well worth the effort. It's a lovely and light twist on classic buttercream, with a smooth texture that's ideal for coating your favorite cakes. It's not as sweet as traditional buttercream, so it makes a tasty substitute for those who prefer their frostings a little less on the sweet side.

Preparation Time: 30 minutes

Portion: Enough to generously fill and cover an 8-inch (20-cm) cake with 3 layers or top at least 12 cupcakes

1¼ cups + 1 tbsp (10½ oz/300 g) unsalted butter

5 large egg whites, room temperature

1 cups (7 oz/200 g) granulated sugar

1 tsp vanilla extract or, for Lemon Swiss Meringue Buttercream (see page 28), the grated zest of 1 lemon

1. Remove the butter from the refrigerator and cut it into cubes. Leave to soften for 15 minutes.

2. Meanwhile, pour a little water into a small pan and place it on the hob. Bring the water to a boil, then reduce the heat and bring the water to a simmer.

3. You'll need a heatproof bowl that you can set on the pan, ensuring the bottom of the bowl does not touch the water beneath it. Put the egg whites and sugar in the bowl and set the bowl on the pan above the simmering water. Whisk the eggs and the sugar in the bowl, keeping the mixture moving to prevent the eggs from cooking. Use a silicone spatula to scrape down the sides of the bowl from time to time, to make sure that all of the sugar is incorporated into the mixture. Insert a candy thermometer into the mixture. When the temperature of the mixture reaches 140ºF (60ºC), which should take approximately 5 minutes, remove the bowl from the heat.

4. Transfer the mixture to the bowl of a stand mixer fitted with a whisk attachment. Whisk at a high speed for 5–10 minutes. The mixture will rise in volume and will become very glossy and quite stiff. Reduce the speed to medium and begin to add your cubed butter pieces, one by one. Make sure that each cube of butter is incorporated before adding the next one.

5. Continue to whisk your buttercream until fluffy. Add your flavoring at this point. The buttercream may look curdled, but keep whisking and it will become pale and fluffy again. If the mixture is looking soupy at this point, pop it into the refrigerator for 5–10 minutes, then return it to the bowl of the stand mixture and continue to whisk. If you find you are still having problems with the texture, add another cube or two of butter and continue to whisk.

Chocolate Ganache

Ganache is one of the best recipes to have up your sleeve if you like to bake cakes. The rich taste of the dark chocolate version or the sweet creaminess of the white chocolate ganache will satisfy the pallet of any chocolate lover. Its texture makes it extremely versatile – it serves as a coating for your cakes, a delicious filling, and also a crumb coat layer on which to apply a fondant covering over a cake, as it sets relatively hard. Use high-quality couverture chocolate for the best results.

Preparation Time: 12 hours (including preparation, setting and bringing to room temperature)

Portion: Enough to fill and cover an 8-inch (20-cm) cake with 3 layers

White Chocolate Ganache

1 lb 4½ oz (580 g) white chocolate
¾ cup + 2 tbsp (7 fl oz/200 ml) heavy cream

Dark Chocolate Ganache

14 oz (400 g) dark chocolate (minimum 50 percent cocoa solids)
1¾ cups (14 fl oz/400 ml) heavy cream

1. Break up the chocolate into small chunks and place these in a heat resistant bowl.

2. Pour the cream into a small pan and heat on the hob over a medium-high heat, stirring with a silicone spatula. When the cream begins to simmer and rise, remove the pan from the heat and pour the cream over your chocolate chunks. Stir the cream and chocolate together with the silicone spatula until they are fully combined (this may take up to 5 minutes). Allow the ganache to cool completely.

3. Once completely cooled, refrigerate overnight to set. Remove from the fridge at least 1 hour before you need to work with it (see box, below) and allow the ganache to come up to room temperature. Keep in an airtight container in the refrigerator for up to 1 week (check the use by dates on your ingredients to ensure they fall within this time scale).

WORKING WITH GANACHE

Ganache must be thick and smooth, but also spreadable (such as the consistency of buttercream) in order for you to be able to use it for your cake. If your ganache is still hard when you want to start using it, scoop out the desired amount and place it in a heat proof bowl. Heat in a microwave oven at high setting in 4-second bursts, stirring between each heating until you have the desired texture. Alternatively, set the bowl on a pan of barely simmering water and stir until the ganache has the desired texture. If it becomes too runny, add a little cool ganache and mix through, or pop it into the fridge for 5–10 minutes.

Techniques

They say a little practise makes perfect, and none of the techniques in this section are particularly difficult to master. When used together, these skills will help you to make the presentation of your cakes that much more impressive and professional looking.

Leveling cakes with a cake-leveling tool

Adjust the wire on your cake-leveling tool to the correct height, so that only the uneven top of your cake will be cut off by the wire. Make sure the wire is completely horizontal. Position the middle of the wire on one side of the cake and, using a sawing motion, cut through the top of the cake to the other side. You can use the same technique to cut a cake horizontally into layers of equal height.

Leveling cakes free-hand

1. Measure up the side of your cake to the height at which you intend to cut off the uneven top. Mark this point by inserting a toothpick into the cake. Now repeat around the sides of the cake at equal distances so that you have several toothpicks marking the cutting height. Four toothpicks will be enough on an 8-inch (20-cm) cake, while a few more toothpicks will be helpful on a larger cake.

2. Gently rest a large serrated knife on a toothpick on one side of the cake, then use it to score a continuous line that travels around the top of your cake directly above all of the toothpicks, ensuring the line is completely horizontal. Once scored, use the knife to cut through your cake at the level of the scored line, removing the toothpicks as you go. You can use the same technique to cut a cake horizontally into layers of equal height.

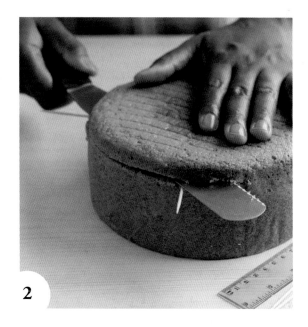

Stacking layers

1. Using a metal spatula, apply a small blob (roughly 1 heaped tsp) of frosting to the center of your cake board or cake plate. Place your first layer of cake onto the cake board or plate. Apply a level layer of frosting across the top of the layer using an angled metal spatula.

2. Apply a second layer of cake on top of the frosting, ensuring it is aligned with the bottom layer. Push down gently but firmly on top to ensure the layer is level. Repeat these steps to stack further layers, then gently push down on the stack to stick the cakes together.

Crumb coating

A crumb coat—a thin layer of frosting—applied to a layer cake traps crumbs, and also provides a good base on which to apply a layer of fondant.

1. Using a metal spatula, apply frosting a little at a time to the sides of your stacked cake. Move the spatula back and forth to spread the frosting in a thin layer across the cake sides, working your way around the entire cake. Because the layer of frosting is applied thinly, it will look patchy. Don't worry—it will be covered with a thicker layer of frosting later.

2. Now apply a thin layer of frosting to the top of the cake in the same way. Refrigerate the cake for up to 30 minutes to allow the crumb coat to set. To test if it has set, touch it with your fingertip—if the buttercream remains intact, the crumb coating has set.

3. You can apply a thicker layer of frosting to the sides and top of the cake over the crumb coat to give the cake a smoother final coating of frosting, or you can leave the crumb coated cake 'naked'. Apply a thicker coating of frosting, then hold the spatula at a 45-degree angle to the side of the cake and use the edge of the spatula to smooth out the frosting. Repeat on the top of the cake.

1

2

3

Covering a cake board with fondant

1. You'll need 1 lb 2 oz (500 g) fondant to cover an 8-inch (20-cm) cake board. Knead the fondant until pliable and soft. Shape it into a ball and smooth out the top. Place the ball, smooth side facing up, on a work surface dusted with confectioner's sugar. Roll out the fondant using a non-stick rolling pin to an even thickness of ⅛ inch (3 mm). Make sure it is large enough to cover your cake board (hover the board over the rolled-out fondant to assess this).

2. Place the cake board on your work surface near the rolled-out fondant. Apply water to the board with a damp paintbrush. Hover the rolling pin above the center of the fondant and carefully flip one side of the fondant over it. Lift up the pin to raise the fondant off the work surface. Roll it out over the board.

3. Gently but firmly press over the surface of the fondant using a cake smoother to smooth it out.

4. Cut away the fondant overhanging the edge of the board with a paring knife, holding the knife upright against the edge and working slowly and carefully. Tidy up the cut edge with a smoother.

5. Give your presentation board a neat finish by wrapping ribbon around its edge. Cut a length of ribbon that's long enough to wrap around the edge of the cake board with a small overlap. Use strips of double-sided tape to apply the ribbon to the edge.

3

1

4

2

5

Covering a cake with fondant

Covering a cake with fondant keeps it fresher for longer. The fondant is a great form of decoration that allows you to experiment with color and design, and forms a good base for edible decorations made using gumpaste. First, apply a crumb coat of buttercream or ganache to your cake (see page 20), then refrigerate the cake for 10–30 minutes until the frosting is firm. Then follow the steps below to give your cake a smooth covering of fondant.

1. You'll need 1 lb 14 oz (850 g) fondant to cover a 3-layer 8-inch (20-cm) round cake. Knead the fondant until smooth and pliable. Roll it into a ball and place this on a work surface dusted with confectioner's sugar, ensuring any creases on the ball of fondant are on the bottom. Use a non-stick rolling pin to roll out the fondant to an even thickness of about ¼ inch (5 mm).

2. Place your rolling pin over the center of the rolled-out fondant and carefully flip one side of the fondant over it. Lift up the pin to raise the fondant off the work surface. Roll it out over your cake, ensuring that the center of the rolled-out fondant is placed over the center of the cake so the fondant can cover both the top and sides of the cake.

3. Using your hand and/or a fondant smoother, smooth out the fondant that's placed over the top of the cake, removing any air bubbles between the cake and fondant by pressing them out to the sides. Now smooth out the fondant on the sides of your cake—cup your hand around one side and smooth the fondant upward, not downward, but working downward from the top of the cake, until the fondant is stuck to the cake.

4. Use a paring knife to cut away excess fondant from around the bottom edges of the cake. Smooth out the fondant all over the cake with a smoother.

2

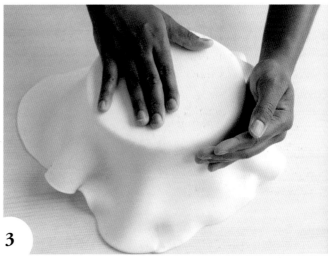

3

4

Applying a smooth ganache coating

1. Crumb coat your cake (see page 20). Using a small spatula, apply ganache a little at a time to the side of your cake, moving the spatula back and forth to spread the ganache in a thick layer. Work your way around the sides of the cake, then apply a layer of ganache to the top of the cake in the same way.

2. Use a dough scraper to lightly scrape down the ganache to create a smooth finish. Hold the dough scraper at a right angle to the side of the cake and then scrape around the circumference of the cake. Add more ganache to any pockets that have been missed by the scraper and scrape down in the same way. You may need to work around the sides of the cake a few times to produce a completely smooth finish. Use the spatula to smooth out the ganache over the top of the cake.

1

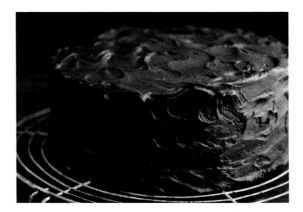

2

Creating a stucco or textured effect

There are two ways to achieve this effect, depending on the type of frosting used. If you are using buttercream, use a metal spatula to apply it thickly to the sides and top of the cake. Press the end of the spatula into the buttercream and pull it away to create peaks in the buttercream coating. With ganache, use the tip of your spatula to make small swirls in the ganache on the surface of your cake. Refrigerate the cake for 10 minutes to allow the frosting to set.

Portioning cupcakes

1. Scoop up some cake batter with an ice cream scoop. Use the blunt side of a kitchen knife to level the scoop, removing excess batter.

2. Release the cake batter from the ice cream scoop directly into a cupcake liner.

Preparing a disposable pastry bag

Cut off the end of your pastry bag to create a hole that's large enough for the point of your piping tip to fit through, but is slightly smaller than the base of the piping tip so that the tip remains attached to the pastry bag. Place the tip into your pastry bag and insert the end of the piping tip through the hole. To fill the bag with the frosting, hold the bag in one hand and fold the ends of it over your hand so you can hold it open easily. Spoon your frosting into the bag until the bag is two-thirds full, using the spoon to push the frosting into the bag to remove any air pockets. Twist the end closed.

Piping swirls on cupcakes

1. Prepare a pastry bag (see opposite page) by fitting it with a star piping tip (for the cupcakes shown in the pictures here, I use a 1M Wilton tip) and filling it with your chosen frosting.

2. To pipe swirls, you'll need to hold the pastry bag in one hand and guide your bag with the other hand, applying pressure to the bag as you pipe. Starting from the outer edge of your cupcake, hold the piping bag 1 inch (2.5 cm) above the cupcake and pipe a continuous line around the outer edge of the cupcake, working your way inward to create a spiral. Overlap the continuous line when you reach the center to finish the swirl. Release pressure on the pastry bag to stop the flow of frosting as you reach the center.

Piping roses

1.

2.

1. Prepare a pastry bag (see opposite page) by fitting it with a star piping tip (for the cake shown in the pictures here, I use a 1M Wilton tip) and filling it with your chosen frosting.

2. Pipe the first rose at the top center of your cake and work outward in a circle from there until you reach the edges. Start at the center of the rose and pipe outward in a spiral to create a rose shape. Pipe

the second rose next to the first in the same way. Continue to pipe roses until you reach the edge of the top of the cake, then begin to pipe your roses down the sides in vertical lines. Once complete, you can fill in any gaps between the roses with small piped stars, made by applying pressure to the pastry bag and then releasing immediately to create a small star shape.

Loaves, Rolls, and Cupcakes

Lemon Meringue Cupcakes

Anyone who suffers periodically from a lemon craving will adore these posh little cupcakes. They are topped with a decadant swirl of lemon meringue frosting and have a secret lemon curd filling for an extra zesty treat.

Preparation Time: 25 minutes, plus baking **|** **Servings:** 12

3½ oz (100 g) lemon curd
12 vanilla cupcakes (see page 11 for recipe, or use store-bought)
1 × batch Lemon Swiss Meringue Buttercream (see page 16)

1. Prepare two pastry bags (see page 24), fitting one with a cupcake filling piping tip (Wilton 230) and the other with a star piping tip (Wilton 1M). Spoon the lemon curd into the bag fitted with the cupcake filling tip, twist and close.

2. Insert the piping tip into the center of a cupcake and squeeze the filling into the cupcake. Be careful not to overfill.

3. Using a small spatula, dab a little lemon curd on the top of each cupcake and spread it out into a thin layer over the top surface.

4. Fill the pastry bag fitted with the star piping tip with the lemon-flavored Swiss meringue buttercream until it is two-thirds of the way full and twist the end closed. Pipe a swirl of frosting (see page 25) onto each cupcake.

2.

4.

You're a Superstar!

With a tangy orange-flavored sponge and cute chocolate star center, there's so much to like about this delicious loaf cake. This design is highly versatile—adapt the colors and flavors to suit the occasion and the palate of your special superstar.

Preparation Time: 35 minutes plus baking, freezing and cooling | **Servings:** 10

1 Chocolate Cake baked in a loaf pan (see page 14)

1 × large batch Classic Vanilla Cake batter (see page 11), flavored with 5 tbsp orange juice plus the grated zest of 1 medium orange in place of the vanilla

½ × batch Swiss Meringue Buttercream (see page 16)

1. Slice the chocolate loaf cake into ten 1-inch (2.5-cm) thick slices. Use a star-shaped cutter with a 2-inch (5-cm) diameter or the star template on page 139 to cut out up to 12 stars from the slices. Place these on a sheet of parchment paper set on a baking sheet and cover with plastic wrap. Freeze on the sheet for 2 hours or until frozen.

2. Preheat the oven to 325°F (160°C). Line a 10 × 5 × 2½ inch (25 × 13 × 6 cm) loaf pan with parchment paper. Pour one-third of the orange-flavored batter into the prepared pan. Place the frozen stars, back to back, in the mix, lining them up along the center of the pan in a tightly packed row. Once aligned, spoon the remaining batter around and over the stars, ensuring they don't move out of alignment.

3. Bake on the middle shelf of the oven for 1 hour or until a cake tester comes out dry. Allow to cool in the pan for 10 minutes, then turn out onto a wire rack and leave to cool completely.

4. Once cooled, turn the loaf right-side up (with the wider side on top). Spread over the Swiss Meringue Buttercream using a spatula. Use a fork to create ridges in the buttercream.

TIP

You can add orange gel food coloring to your cake batter for a pop of color and to highlight the orange flavor of the cake.

2a.

2b.

Popping Candy Cupcakes

It's up to you whether to warn your guests when you offer them these loaded cupcakes or leave them in the dark about the explosive filling, so you can witness the surprise on their faces. If, like me, you have a naughty streak, you'll probably opt for the latter. Serve these crazy cupcakes as soon as they are made for best results.

Preparation Time: 25 minutes plus baking | **Servings:** 12

12 vanilla cupcakes (see page 11 for a recipe, or use store-bought)
3½ oz (100 g) Pop Rocks
1 × batch Classic Buttercream (see page 15)

1. Hold a cupcake on your work surface. Gently push the edge of a round cookie cutter that's approximately 1.5–2 inches (4–5 cm) in diameter into the centre of the top of the cupcake until it is inserted. Holding the cutter in place, gently twist the cupcake and apply pressure, so that you are cutting into the cupcake. Once the cutter is about halfway in, gently twist it and pull the cutter out. Remove the cut-out section of cake from the cutter and set aside. Repeat with the remaining cupcakes.

2. Fill the hole created in the cupcake with 1 heaped teaspoon of popping candy. Replace the cut-out section of cake, pushing it down to fit back into place (don't worry if the cake cracks on top—it will be covered with frosting). Repeat with the remaining cupcakes.

3. Prepare a pastry bag (see page 24) and fit it with a star piping tip (Wilton 1M). Fill the bag with the buttercream until it is two-thirds full, then twist the end closed. Pipe a swirl (see page 25) onto the top of each cupcake.

TIP

If you cannot find a circle cutter, try using the base end of a piping tip to cut the recesses in the cupcakes.

1.

2.

Chocolate Bean Cupcakes

Sugar-coated chocolate beans inside a scrumptious chocolate cupcake… is that a yes? Then these are the perfect cupcakes for you. They're packed with chocolately goodness and are designed to please the serious chocolate lover.

Preparation Time: 25 minutes plus baking | **Servings:** 12

12 chocolate cupcakes (see page 14 for a recipe, or use store-bought)

5½ oz (150 g) plain M&Ms

1 × batch Classic Buttercream, flavored with chocolate in place of vanilla (see pages 15 and 10)

1. Hold a cupcake on your work surface. Gently push the edge of a round cookie cutter that's approximately 1.5–2 inches (4–5 cm) in diameter into the centre of the top of the cupcake until it is inserted *(see the picture for step 1 on page 32, which shows this technique).* Holding the cutter in place, gently twist the cupcake and apply pressure to cut into the cupcake. Once the cutter is about halfway in, gently twist it and pull the cutter out. Remove the cut-out section of cake from the cutter and set aside.

2. Fill the hole created in the cupcake with a generous amount of M&Ms (7–8 per cupcake should do the trick). Replace the cut-out cake, pushing it down to fit back into place (don't worry if the cake cracks on top, it will be covered with frosting). Repeat steps 1 and 2 with the remaining cupcakes.

3. Prepare a pastry bag (see page 24), fitting it with a star piping tip (Wilton 1M) and filling it with the chocolate buttercream. Pipe a swirl (see page 25) onto the top of each cupcake.

Little Planets

Impressive on the outside, surprising on the inside, these delicious and moreish cake balls are perfect for a child's birthday party. Have fun dipping the balls and creating your own worlds, and let the guests find out what's at the core of your planet—cake!

Preparation Time: 45 minutes plus baking and freezing | **Servings:** 12

12 vanilla cupcakes, 6 colored
    red (see page 11 for a recipe,
    or use store-bought)
4 tbsp Classic Buttercream
    (see page 15)
7 oz (200 g) white chocolate
4 tbsp vegetable oil
Gel food colors in green
    and blue

1. Break up the cupcakes into crumbs, keeping the red crumbs in one bowl and the uncolored cupcake crumbs in another bowl.

2. Add 1–2 tablespoons of buttercream to the bowl containing the uncolored cake crumbs and mix together to form a dough. Roll the dough into 12 balls, each with a diameter of approximately 1 inch (2.5 cm). Place the balls on a piece of parchment paper set on a baking sheet and cover with plastic wrap. Freeze on the sheet for 30 minutes.

3. Mix the remaining buttercream into the red cake crumbs to create a red dough. Take the frozen balls out of the freezer. Divide the red dough in the bowl into 12 equal portions. Taking 1 portion, create a large dough ball, then flatten it out in your palm until it is about ¼ inch (5 mm) thick. Place one of the frozen balls in the center of this shape and carefully envelope the frozen ball in the red dough (*see picture on page 38*). Make sure that all of the vanilla cake ball is covered in red dough, which should be molded around the ball inside so that the whole thing looks spherical. Place the covered ball

2a.

2b.

3.

5.

❧ *Loaves, Rolls, and Cupcakes* ❧

on a piece of parchment paper set on a baking sheet, then repeat the process with the remaining frozen balls and portions of red dough. Cover the balls with plastic wrap, then freeze on the baking sheet for 1 hour.

4. Break the white chocolate into pieces and place 5½ oz (150 g) in one bowl and 1½ oz (50 g) in another bowl. Melt the chocolate in a microwave oven in 30 second bursts using the highest heat setting. Once runny, add 3 tbsp vegetable oil to the larger portion and 1 tbsp to the smaller portion and mix thoroughly (this will make the chocolate extra runny). Color the larger portion blue and the smaller portion green using gel food colors.

5. Remove the balls from the freezer and pierce each one with a toothpick, inserting it halfway into the ball. Dip each ball into the blue-colored melted chocolate. Gently tap the toothpick against the top of the bowl, knocking off any excess chocolate. This coating of blue is the 'sea' on your little planet. Remove the toothpick, using a teaspoon to help you, and place the completed ball on a cookie sheet lined with baking parchment. Repeat with the remaining balls. If the balls start to become soft, return them to the freezer for 5–10 minutes. Once all the balls are decorated, pop the sheet into the freezer and freeze the cake balls for 10 minutes.

6. Once hardened, use a toothpick to spread some green melted chocolate onto the blue, creating land on your planets. Pop the balls back into the freezer for a final 10 minutes before serving. These can be kept in the refrigerator for up to one week if you are not serving them immediately.

PB and J Cupcakes

Love peanut butter? Love strawberry jelly? Love them mixed together? These cupcakes are a twist on the classic sandwich and are a must for peanut butter lovers. With just the right amount of jelly to balance the stickiness of the peanut butter, one of these makes the perfect little treat.

Preparation Time: 25 minutes plus baking | **Servings:** 12

1¾ oz (50 g) strawberry jelly

1¾ oz (50 g) peanut butter

12 vanilla cupcakes (see page 11 for a recipe, or use store-bought)

1 × batch Classic Buttercream (see page 15)

Handful of crushed peanuts, to decorate

1. Prepare 3 pastry bags (see page 24), fitting 2 with a cupcake filling piping tip (Wilton 230) and 1 with a star piping tip (Wilton 1M). Spoon the jelly into one of the bags fitted with a filling tip and the peanut butter into the other. Twist each bag to close.

2. Take one of the pastry bags fitted with a cupcake filling tip, insert the tip into the center of the cupcake and squeeze the filling into the cupcake. Be careful not to overfill. Now repeat with the other filling. Repeat with the remaining cupcakes.

3. Using a small spatula, dab a little jelly on the top of each cupcake and spread it out into a thin layer over the top surface.

4. Spoon the buttercream into the pastry bag fitted with the star piping tip until it is two-thirds full, then twist the end closed. Pipe a swirl (see page 25) onto the top of each cupcake.

5. To finish, sprinkle each cupcake with crushed peanuts.

TIP

Squeeze some peanut butter and jelly out of the pastry bags onto paper towels. You will then be able to see how much filling will be added to your cupcakes with each squeeze, and estimate how hard and how long to squeeze the bags for in order to get the right amount of fillings into your cupcakes.

Hazelnutty Cupcakes

I first made these cupcakes for my friend Sarah's birthday party. She loves the flavor of hazelnuts and is obsessed with chocolate. Be ready when serving these rich and decadent treats—they are extremely moreish, so you may need more than you think!

Preparation Time: 25 minutes plus baking | **Servings:** 12

5½ oz (150 g) hazelnut spread

12 chocolate cupcakes (see page 14 for a recipe, or use store-bought)

1 × batch Classic Buttercream (see page 15)

1 cup (3½ oz/100 g) chopped hazelnuts

1. Prepare 2 pastry bags (see page 24), fitting 1 with a cupcake filling piping tip (Wilton 230) and the other with a star piping tip (Wilton 1M). Spoon all but 1 tbsp of the hazelnut spread into the bag fitting with the cupcake filling tip, twist and close.

2. Insert the filling tip into the center of a cupcake and squeeze the filling into the cupcake. Be careful not to overfill. Repeat with the remaining cupcakes and hazelnut spread.

3. Using a small spatula, dab a little hazelnut spread on the top of each cupcake and spread it out into a thin layer over the top surface.

4. Mix the vanilla buttercream with the reserved 1 tbsp of hazelnut spread. Place the hazelnut buttercream into the pastry bag fitted with the star piping tip until it is two-thirds full, then twist the end closed. Pipe a swirl (see page 25) onto the top of each cupcake.

5. To finish, top each cupcake with a sprinkling of chopped hazelnuts.

Striped Swiss Roll

Deliciously simple to make and oh-so-colorful, this stripy treat is enough to brighten anyone's day. If you are feeling particularly adventurous, add some gel food coloring to the heavy cream before whipping for a mind-bogglingly colorful dessert.

Preparation Time: 45 minutes plus baking and cooling | **Servings:** 10

½ cup + 2 tbsp (4½ oz/125 g) superfine sugar

4 large eggs, at room temperature

1 cup + 2 tbsp (4½ oz/125 g) all-purpose flour

1¼ cups (10 fl oz/300 ml) heavy cream, whipped until thick

Gel food colors in pink and purple

TIP

Rolling up your cake as soon as it comes out of the oven will help you to re-roll it effectively later. The cake is still flexible when it is hot, so will take the shape without the sponge cracking too much. Make sure you roll it up slowly and tightly. And ensure it is completely cool before you first unroll it.

1. Preheat the oven to 375ºF (190ºC). Line a jellyroll pan or baking sheet that's roughly 14 × 9 inches (35 × 23 cm) with parchment paper.

2. Whisk the sugar and eggs in an electric stand mixer set to a medium speed until pale in color and thick in texture. The mixture should double in size, which may take up to 5 minutes.

3. Sift half of the flour into the egg mixture and fold it in using a metal spoon. Add the other half in one go and continue to fold in the flour. Be sure not to over-fold the mixture.

4. Divide the mixture into two equal portions. Add purple food gel coloring to 1 portion and pink food gel coloring to the other. Gently fold in the color and stop mixing as soon as the color is incorporated. Spoon each portion of the mixture into a separate disposable pastry bag (*see picture on page 46*).

5. Cut off the tip of one bag and pipe the mixture onto the prepared pan in diagonal stripes, keeping them as straight as possible and leaving space between each stripe for stripes of the other color (*see picture on page 46*). Now repeat the process, filling the gaps between the stripes with stripes of the other color to make a pattern of alternating stripes on the parchment paper (*see picture on page 46*).

6. Bake for 10–12 minutes until the center of the sponge bounces back when touched. Dampen a dish towel with cold water and place it on top of the cake. Flip it over (use a dry dish towel to handle the cookie sheet as this will be hot) to remove the cake from the pan.

4.

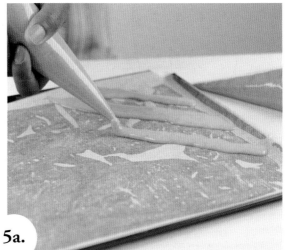

5a.

5b.

7.

8.

10.

7. Gently and slowly peel away the parchment paper. Place another damp dish towel over the top of your cake and flip it over so that the brighter side of the cake (which was facing into the pan during baking) is facing downward. Tightly roll up the cake in the damp dish towel so that the dish towel is rolled up in the cake (which helps it to cool down). Leave to cool for at least 30 minutes.

8. Once cooled, unroll the cake and dish towel. Using a spatula, spread half the whipped cream across the exposed surface, starting from the middle area and spreading outward toward the edges until the cream is ½ inch (1 cm) from the edge. The cream should be approximately ¼ inch (5 mm) thick.

9. Now roll up the cake over the filling at one end along the shorter width, rolling away from you.

10. Place the rolled-up cake onto some parchment paper, positioning the seam at the bottom of the cake, and spread the remaining cream over the top and sides. This will conceal the surprise inside. Pop the roll into the refrigerator for 1 hour to allow it to set before serving.

Celebration Cakes

—◆—

Rainbow Surprise

*It may be simple in its design, but this cake is impressive in its execution and provides
a very elegant way in which to brighten up any event.*

Preparation Time: 1 hour plus baking and chilling | **Servings:** 12

**2 × batches Classic Buttercream
(see page 15)**
**Gel food colors in red, orange,
yellow, green, blue, and
purple**
**4 × 8-inch (20-cm) round
White Cake sandwich layers
(see page 13), each leveled
and cut into 2 layers (discard
1 layer to leave you with 7)**

1. Spoon 2–3 heaped tablespoons of buttercream into each of
6 bowls. Use a gel food color to give each portion a strong, bright hue.

2. Place a small blob of uncolored buttercream onto a 10-inch
(25-cm) cake plate and position the first layer of your white sponge
cake in the center. Use an angled metal spatula to spread the purple
buttercream over the top of the cake layer, smoothing it to the edge
and keeping it level. Place another cake layer on top and push down
to secure it in place. Spread over the blue buttercream and repeat,
placing another layer of cake on top, then moving on to green, then
yellow, then orange, and finishing with a layer of red buttercream.
Place the final cake layer on top, pressing down to ensure the entire
cake tower is level.

3. Crumb coat the cake (see page 20) with the remaining uncolored
buttercream. Refrigerate for 30 minutes to allow the frosting to set
(you may need to remove some shelves in your refrigerator to make
space for a cake this tall).

4. Cover the cake generously with the remaining uncolored
buttercream. To finish, place the flat tip of a metal spatula at the
bottom of the side of the cake and pull it upward, making an
indentation in the buttercream. Work your way around the cake until
the cake is decorated with vertical lines all the way around the sides.
Now move on to the top of the cake. Start from the top edge of the
cake and, using the same technique, pull the metal spatula toward the
center of the top, working your way around the top until complete.

Berry Explosion

This beautiful cake is always a hit at special events and makes a perfect wedding cake. Its core bursts with fresh berries, the unfussy 'naked' presentation is very graceful, and a sprinkling of confectioner's sugar adds a touch of elegance.

Preparation Time: 1–2 hours | **Servings:** 8–10

3 × 8-inch (20-cm) round Classic Vanilla Cake sandwich layers (see page 11), leveled
1 × batch Classic Buttercream (see page 15)
7 oz (200 g) assorted fresh berries (such as blueberries, raspberries, and currents)
Confectioner's sugar, to sprinkle

1. Using a 3-inch (7-cm) round cookie cutter, remove the center from each of your cake layers. Discard the cut-out centers. You will be left with 3 cake rings.

2. Smear some buttercream onto a 10-inch (25-cm) cake plate. Place a cake layer in the center of the plate—the buttercream will stick the cake to the plate. Now spread a layer of buttercream across the top of the cake layer using an angled metal spatula, smoothing the frosting to the edges and keeping it level. Make sure that no buttercream is smeared into the hole. Place another cake layer on top and push down to secure it in place, ensuring the holes in the middle are aligned. Spread on more buttercream and apply the final cake layer, pressing down to make sure the cake is level.

3. Use buttercream to neatly crumb coat the cake (see page 20) around the sides.

4. Mix your berries gently by hand and pour them into the well in the center of the cake until it is full. Neatly crumb coat the top of the cake, then place some berries on top. To finish, sprinkle with a little confectioner's sugar.

Psychedelic Chic

This party cake has a stylish understated exterior, but when you cut it, your guests will really know it's party time! A magnificently vibrant interior is given a gorgeous wow-factor with a swirling marble of bold and bright colors. The effect is fantastic, yet is very simple to achieve. Choose colors that contrast for the most outstanding results.

Preparation Time: 45 minutes plus baking and cooling | **Servings:** 8–10

1 × **medium batch White Cake batter (see page 13)**
Gel food colors in yellow, orange, red, purple, and green
1 × **batch Classic Buttercream (see page 15)**

1. Preheat the oven to 325ºF (160ºC). Line an 8-inch (20-cm) round cake pan with parchment paper. Divide the cake batter into 5 equal portions in separate bowls. Mix a different food coloring into each bowl, mixing the color through using a whisk or tablespoon.

2. Spoon the colored batters into your cake pan, alternating the colors as you add them and ensuring the different colors of batter are overlapping *(see picture 2 on page 61, which shows this technique)*. Then tap the cake pan 2–3 times on the work surface in order to level out the batter.

3. Insert a dinner knife into the batter at a 90-degree angle until it touches the bottom of the pan. Keeping the knife at this angle, swirl it inside the batter, dragging the colors into each other to marble them. Avoid overmixing so the colors do not blend together, but are instead marbled through one another.

4. Bake for 50 minutes or until a cake tester comes out clean. Allow the cake to cool in the pan for 10 minutes, then turn it out onto a wire rack and leave to cool completely.

5. Color the buttercream with yellow gel food coloring. Place the cake on a 10-inch (25-cm) cake plate and use the yellow buttercream to crumb coat your cake (see page 20). Refrigerate for 30 minutes to allow the frosting to set.

6. To finish, cover the cake generously with a layer of buttercream.

Polka Dot Cake

This deceptively simple cake uses the twice-baked method. You will need a silicone cake pop mold for this design. These are readily available from specialist suppliers. I have chosen four bright colors, but you can choose any combinations of colors you like. It's a great project for children's birthday parties, or for those that are still young at heart.

Preparation Time: 1 hour 15 minutes plus baking, overnight drying, and freezing | **Servings:** 8–10

2 lb 4 oz (1 kg) white ready-to-use fondant

Confectioner's sugar, to dust

2 × large batches Classic Vanilla Cake batter (see page 11)

Food gel colors in pink, green, blue, and orange

1 × batch White Chocolate Ganache (see page 17)

3½ oz (100 g) white gumpaste

1. First, use some of the white fondant to cover a 10-inch (25-cm) round cake board (see page 21). You'll need 1 yard (1 m) of orange ribbon. Wrap it around the edge of the cake board and secure it with strips of double-sided tape. Leave the covered cake board out overnight to allow it to dry.

2. Preheat the oven to 325ºF (160ºC). Spoon 3 tbsp of the batter into each of 4 bowls. Color the batter in each bowl with a different food coloring.

3. Place the bottom half of your cake pop mold on a baking sheet and generously spray each pocket with cake release spray. Spoon the colored batter into the pockets, filling to the top ridge (*see picture on page 59*). Once full, press the top half of the mold onto the bottom half, ensuring it is secured tightly. Bake for 25 minutes.

4. Remove the mold from the oven, peel away the top half of the mold, then place the bottom half (containing the cake pops) on a wire rack to cool for 10 minutes. Now remove each cake ball carefully from the mold. Using a paring knife, carve away any excess cake around the central edges (*see picture on page 59*), then leave the cake balls on the rack to cool completely.

5. Place the balls on a piece of parchment paper on a baking sheet and cover with plastic wrap, then freeze for 2 hours or until frozen.

6. Line two 8-inch (20-cm) round cake pans with parchment paper. Take the cake balls out of the freezer. Pour enough of the vanilla cake batter into each of the prepared pans to cover the bottoms of the pans.

Place the cake balls in the cake batter in the pans, spacing them about 1 inch (2.5 cm) apart and alternating the colors where possible (you can fit approximately 8 balls in each pan). Gently spoon the remaining vanilla cake batter around and over the balls (ensure you don't move them out of place) until the balls are only just covered. Bake for 50 minutes or until a cake tester comes out clean. Cool in the pans for 10 minutes, then turn out the cakes onto a wire rack and allow to cool completely.

7. Place a small amount of white chocolate ganache onto the center of your prepared cake board. Position the first layer centrally on the board, then spread over some white chocolate ganache. Align the second cake layer on top. Crumb coat the entire cake (see page 20) using the white chocolate ganache. Refrigerate the cake for 10 minutes to allow the frosting to set.

8. Use the remaining white fondant to cover the cake (see page 22).

9. To finish, cut your gumpaste in 4 equal pieces and color each piece using the same food colors used to color the cake balls. Roll out each section, one by one, to a thickness of roughly ⅛ inch (3 mm). Use a round cookie cutter with a diameter of about 1½ inches (4 cm) to cut out circles in different colors. Attach these to the top and sides of your cake using a dampened paintbrush.

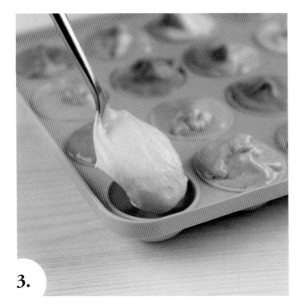

3.

4.

6.

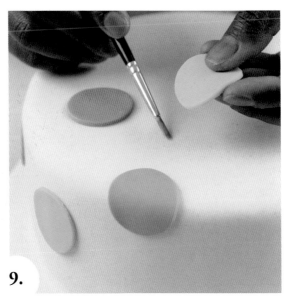

9.

Camouflage Cake

Hidden within this scrumptious chocolate-covered cake are the classic camouflage colors, whorling in swirly stripes and blobs. This design is great for a boy's or action-girl's birthday party. Use the recipe to make cupcakes for a cute mini variation.

Preparation Time: 45 minutes plus baking and cooling | **Servings:** 8–10

1 × **large batch Classic Vanilla Cake batter (see page 11)**
Gel food color in khaki
2 tbsp **unsweetened cocoa powder**
½ × **batch Dark Chocolate Ganache (see page 17)**

1. Preheat the oven to 325ºF (160ºC). Line an 8-inch (20-cm) round cake pan with parchment paper. Divide the cake batter into 3 equal portions in separate bowls. Mix some khaki food coloring into the batter in one bowl and the cocoa powder in to the batter in another bowl.

2. Spoon heaped tablespoons of each batter into the prepared baking pan, alternating the 2 colored portions and the uncoloured one as you add them. Do this so that the different colors overlap. Once all the batter is spooned into the cake pan, tap the pan on the work surface 2–3 times in order to level out the surface of the batter.

3. Bake for 1 hour and 10 minutes or until a cake tester comes out clean. Allow to cool in the pan for 10 minutes, then turn it out onto a wire rack and allow to cool completely.

4. Position the cake on a 10-inch (25-cm) cake plate. Use a spatula to apply a crumb coating (see page 20) of the ganache onto the cake, then refrigerate for 10 minutes to set. Now apply a generous layer of ganache to the cake. Smooth the edges using a dough scraper (see page 23). Refrigerate for 10 minutes to allow the ganache to set before serving.

1.　**2.**

What's in a Cake?

How amazing would it be to find your name inside a cake that has been presented to you? It would be pretty awesome, if you ask me! The only question is, if the name inside the cake is yours, are you still obliged to share?

Preparation Time: 1 hour 15 minutes plus baking, overnight drying, and freezing | **Servings:** 15–20

2 lb 4 oz (1 kg) white ready-to-use fondant

Confectioner's sugar, to dust

2 × Chocolate Cakes baked in a loaf pan (see page 14)—for names spelled with more than 4 letters, you may need an additional loaf

1 × large batch Classic Vanilla Cake batter (see page 11)

½ × batch Classic Buttercream (see page 15)

1¾ oz (50 g) brown gumpaste

1. You'll need a 10-inch (25-cm) square cake board for this project. Cover it with white fondant (see page 21). To finish the board presentation you'll need roughly a yard of brown ribbon—wrap it around the edge of the board and secure it to the board using strips of double-sided tape. Leave the fondant-covered board out overnight to allow it to dry.

2. Slice each of your chocolate loaf cakes into 10 equal slices, each with a thickness of about 1 inch (2.5 cm).

3. You'll need letter-shaped cookie cutters to spell out the name you are baking into your cake. Spell a name with a maximum of 6 letters for full effect (perhaps a nickname can be used for longer names). The size of the letter cookie cutters required depends on the number of letters in the name. Hold the cookie cutters against the side of the pan and map out their rough placement across one side of the pan to make sure the name will fit across the width of the pan. Now use your cutters to cut out the name from the slices of chocolate cake. You'll need roughly 8 cut outs of each letter in the name. Place the cut outs on a sheet of parchment paper set on a baking sheet and cover with plastic wrap. Freeze for 2 hours or until frozen.

4. Towards the end of the freezing time, preheat the oven to 325ºF (160ºC). Line 8-inch (20-cm) square cake pan with parchment paper.

5. Remove the letters from the freezer. For this cake, you'll be using the same technique as shown on page 31 to form the name inside the cake. Pour enough of the cake batter into the prepared pan to cover the bottom. Now place the letters inside the mix. So, for example, if you were to spell out the name John, position a line of Js, back to back in a tightly packed row, at the left side of the pan *(see picture on page 31, which shows this technique)*. Slightly to the right of this row of Js, position a row of Os, followed by a row of Hs, then a row of Ns at the right side of the pan. Try to position the rows of letters so that the spacing between the letters is equal. Spoon the remaining cake batter into a pastry bag and snip off the end. Pipe the cake batter around and over the letters, ensuring you don't move them out of place. Insert a toothpick into the batter to mark the front of your cake. Note that the letters may rise during baking (as they have in the picture on the previous page), which creates a charming effect, but if you prefer the letters to be at the same level within the cake, gently tap the pan on your work surface to release any air bubbles trapped in the batter, then prick these with a toothpick when they rise to the surface.

6. Bake on the middle shelf of the oven for 1 hour and 10 minutes or until a cake tester comes out dry. Allow to cool in the pan for 10 minutes, then turn out onto a wire rack to cool completely. Reposition the toothpick as necessary so that it still indicates which side is the front of your cake.

7. Once cooled, turn over the cake so that the top is uppermost. Use the vanilla buttercream to apply a crumb coat (see page 20), then refrigerate for 30 minutes to set. Meanwhile, roll out the brown gumpaste and cut out roughly 15 of each letter that spells out the name using smaller letter cutters. Set aside.

8. Remove the toothpick from the front of your cake and cover the cake with a layer of white fondant (see page 22). Make a discrete mark in the fondant at the bottom of the cake to indicate which is the front. To finish, use a dampened paintbrush to apply the gumpaste letters to the top and sides of the cake to spell out the name several times. Make sure that, when you cut the cake, you cut it from side to side, not front to back, so that the name is revealed.

Soccerball Cake

This cake is sure to delight soccer fans. The fun design of the exterior conjures a soccer pitch, and then when the cake is sliced, a bunch of chocolate soccer balls just roll on out, adding a touch of excitement to this party treat.

Preparation Time: 1 hour 30 minutes plus overnight drying, baking, and cooling | **Servings:** 6–8

7 oz (200 g) green ready-to-use fondant

Confectioner's sugar, to dust

1 × small batch Classic Vanilla Cake batter (see page 11)

20 foiled chocolate soccer balls

¼ × batch Classic Buttercream (see page 15)

1 lb 2 oz (500 g) white ready-to-use fondant

3½ oz (100 g) black gumpaste

Gel food color in green

1. Cover a round 10-inch (25-cm) cake board with green fondant (see page 21). You'll need 1 yard (1 m) of green ribbon. Wrap it around the edge of the board and secure it with strips of double-sided tape. Leave the covered cake board out overnight to dry.

2. Preheat the oven to 325ºF (160ºC). You'll need a dome-shaped cake pan or a heatproof glass bowl with a 6-inch (15-cm) diameter in which to bake the cake. Prepare the pan or bowl by spraying the inside with cake-release spray. Pour in the cake batter, filling the pan or bowl two-thirds of the way to the rim. Bake on the middle shelf of the oven for 30 minutes or until a cake tester comes out dry. Cool in the pan or bowl for 10 minutes, then turn out onto a wire rack to cool completely.

3. Once the cake is cool, gently hold it by the dome and, using a paring knife, carve out a dome-shaped hollow in the center of the flat plane, ensuring you leave a 1-inch (2.5-cm) border around the edge of the hollow. You want to carve only halfway into the cake. Remove the excess cake and crumbs and discard.

4. Carefully position the domed side of your cake on a work surface and place the chocolate soccer balls inside, ensuring not to overfill the hollow—the soccer balls should be level with the flat surface of the cake. If you like, you can apply some buttercream to the border around the hollow at this stage, using an angled metal spatula, which will help to stick the cake to the board. Position the covered cake board, face down, on top of the cake, with the circular edge of the cake positioned centrally under the circular cake board (*see picture on page 67*). Holding both the cake and board together, flip the whole lot over. The cake will now be on top of the board (*see picture on page 67*).

5. Crumb coat the cake (see page 20) using roughly 3 heaped tbsps of the buttercream, then refrigerate for 30 minutes to set.

6. Remove the cake from the refrigerator, then roll out the white fondant and use it to cover the cake (see page 22).

7. Roll out the black gumpaste to a thickness of ⅛ inch (3 mm). Using the pentagon-shaped template on page 139, cut out 5 pentagons from the gumpaste. Using a dampened paintbrush, stick these to the cake, placing 1 on top and 4, equally spaced, around the sides of the cake, as shown in the picture below.

8. Mix some green food coloring into the remaining buttercream. Prepare a pastry bag (see page 24), fitting it with a grass piping tip (Wilton 233). Fill the bag with the green buttercream, then pipe grass onto the cake board around the edges of the cake. If you like, you can place some chocolate soccer balls onto the edge of the grass for decoration to finish.

4a.

4b.

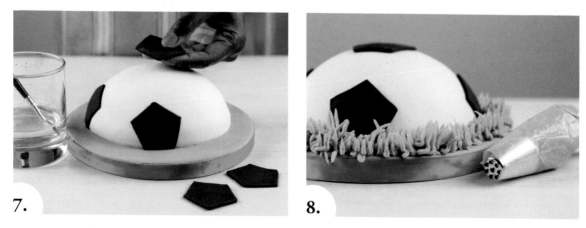

7.

8.

Zebra Cake

This cake is inspired by my sister, Jenna, who likes to test my skills on her birthday cakes and often asks for something a bit crazy on the inside. This cake is a tribute to her alternative and creative nature. We like pink, but feel free to experiment with the colors on this rather fabulous design.

Preparation Time: 1 hour plus overnight drying, baking, and cooling | **Servings:** 8–10

2 lb 4 oz (1 kg) bright pink ready-to-use fondant
Confectioner's sugar
1 × large batch White Cake batter (see page 13)
Gel food colours in pink and black
1 × batch Classic Buttercream (see page 15)

1. You'll need a 10-inch (25-cm) round cake board for this project. Cover it with some of the bright pink fondant (see page 21). To finish the board presentation you'll need roughly 1 yard (1 m) of black ribbon—wrap it around the edge of the board and secure it to the board using strips of double-sided tape. Leave the covered board out overnight to allow it to dry.

2. Preheat the oven to 325ºF (160ºC). Line 3 × 8-inch (20-cm) round sandwich cake pans with parchment paper.

3. Spoon half of the cake batter into a separate bowl. Set one portion aside—this will remain uncolored. Take the other portion and transfer one-third of its contents into a third bowl. Color the larger of these 2 portions with black food coloring and the smaller portion with pink food coloring. Ensure each batter is thoroughly mixed with its color.

4. Spoon 2 tbsp of white (uncolored) batter into the center of a prepared cake pan (*see picture on page 71*). On top of and in the center of this circle of batter, spoon approximately ½ tbsp of pink batter (*see picture on page 71*). Next, spoon 1 tbsp of black batter into the center of the pink mix (*see picture on page 71*). (The pink mix may become obscured by the black, but this is okay).

5. Continue with this method—adding 2 tbsp white, ½ tbsp pink, then 1 tbsp black batter, one spoonful on top of the next—until the batter touches the sides of the pan (*see pictures on page 71*). If the batter touches one side of the pan before the other, gently tilt and shake the pan so that it fills the whole space. End with 1 tbsp of white mix in the center. Repeat this process in the other two prepared cake pans using the remaining batter.

6. Place the pans in the oven—if you can fit all three, great, but if you can't, bake two, then bake the third separately. Bake for 30 minutes or until a cake tester comes out clean. Allow the cakes to cool in the pans for 10 minutes, then turn out onto a wire rack and leave them to cool completely.

7. If necessary, level the tops of your cake layers (see page 18–19). Now stack the layers on your fondant-covered cake board, using buttercream to stick the first layer to the board, then applying a layer of buttercream between each layer. Crumb coat the cake (see page 20) with the remaining buttercream. Refrigerate for 30 minutes to allow the frosting to set.

8. Cover the cake with the remaining fondant (see page 22). To make the beaded edge, roll small pieces of pink fondant in your hand to make balls. Stick these to the cake board around the sides of your cake using a dampened paintbrush.

4a.

4b.

4c.

5a.

5b.

5c.

5d.

5e.

Fairy Dust Cake

If you know a little girl who likes fairies, princesses, and all things pink, this is the ideal cake for her birthday party. Watching the awe on little faces as the cake is cut and the 'fairy dust' pours out is priceless. Magic comes included in recipe…

Preparation Time: 1 hour 30 minutes plus overnight drying, baking, and cooling | **Servings:** 10–12

2 lb 4 oz (1 kg) pink ready-to-use fondant

Confectioner's sugar, to dust

9 oz (250 g) yellow gumpaste

2 × 6-inch (15-cm) Classic Vanilla Cakes (see page 11), each leveled and cut into 2 layers

1 × batch White Chocolate Ganache (see page 17)

9 oz (250 g) pink glimmer sugar crystals

TOP TIP

You can use edible gold paint and a food-only paint brush to paint the tiara and wand gold. Allow the paint to dry completely before positioning them with the cake.

---

1. Use some of the pink fondant to cover a 10-inch (25-cm) round cake board (see page 21). You'll need 1 yard (1 m) of pink ribbon. Wrap it around the edge of the cake board and secure it with strips of double-sided tape. Leave the covered cake board out overnight to allow it to dry.

2. Prepare the tiara and wand the night before you bake the cake. Dust your work surface with confectioner's sugar, then roll out some of the yellow gumpaste to a thickness of ½ inch (1 cm). Use a star-shaped cookie cutter to cut out a star shape (*see picture on page 74*). Set aside. Using the remaining gumpaste, roll 4 long, thin sausage shapes. Use a small saucepan or a round cake pan with a diameter of roughly 5 inches (13 cm) as a shape former. Wrap one sausage shape around the pot—this will form the base of your tiara (*see picture on page 74*). Cut the second sausage shape in half and shape each half into a spiral. Using a dampened paintbrush, attach the spirals to the center of the tiara base (*see picture on page 74*) so that the spirals are mirror images of each other. Create a heart shape with the third sausage shape that will fit between the two spirals. Allow the heart shape to dry on a flat surface overnight (so that it doesn't lose its shape)—you can attach it the next day using a dampened paintbrush. Insert a toothpick halfway into the fourth sausage and push your pre-cut star onto it, adhering with a small amount of water (*see picture on page 74*). Leave all of these gumpaste shapes out overnight to set.

3. The following day, attach the heart shape to the top of the tiara using a dampened paintbrush and allow to set for at least 1 hour.

2a.

2b.

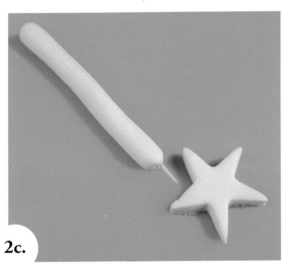

2c.

4.

5.

6.

4. Using a 2-inch (5-cm) round cookie cutter, remove the centers from 2 of your 4 cake layers to form 2 cake rings. Discard the cut-out cake centers.

5. Using an angled metal spatula, apply a small amount of white chocolate ganache to the prepared cake board and position an uncut cake layer centrally on the board. Apply a thin layer of ganache to the top of the cake layer, avoiding the central area that will form the bottom of the central well, then align a cake ring on top. Apply a thin layer of ganache to the top of the cake ring (make sure there is no ganache in the central well), then align the second ring on top.

6. Pour the pink glimmer sugar crystals into the well in the center of the cake until they reach the top. Spread some white chocolate ganache onto the top ring and stick the final cake layer to the top, enclosing the sugar crystals.

7. Crumb coat the sides and the top of the cake (see page 20) with the white chocolate ganache, then refrigerate for 10 minutes to set.

8. Roll out the remaining pink fondant into a circle with a diameter of approximately 12 inches (30 cm) and a thickness of ¼ inch (5 mm) and use this to cover the top and sides of the cake (see page 22). Use a smoother and your hands to smooth the fondant onto the cake.

9. To finish, carefully place the wand on the board to the side of the cake, and position the tiara either overlapping the side of the board, alongside the wand, or on top of the cake.

> **TIP**
>
> If you can't get hold of sugar crystals, you can fill the cake with colored sugar. Place 9 oz (250 g) white sugar in a bowl and add 5–6 drops of liquid food coloring. Mix it in thoroughly with a fork until all the crystals are colored. Spread out the sugar on parchment paper and allow to dry for at least 1 hour. Place the sugar in a bowl and mix again, breaking up any clumps that may have formed. The granules will be smaller than store-bought sugar crystals, but the effect is still lovely!

Leopard Print Cake

This funky cake is simple to make, but the feral design is sure to impress! Express your wild side with this tempting and striking cake.

Preparation Time: 1 hour 30 minutes plus overnight drying, baking, and cooling | **Servings:** 8–10

1 × **large batch Classic Vanilla Cake batter (see page 11)**

Gel food color in orange

2 tbsp unsweetened cocoa powder

1 × **batch Classic Buttercream (see page 15)**

1¾ oz (50 g) pale brown gumpaste

1¾ oz (50 g) dark brown gumpaste

1 lb 2 oz (500 g) orange ready-to-use fondant

Confectioner's sugar, to dust

1. Use some of the orange fondant to cover a 10-inch (25-cm) round cake board (see page 22). You'll need 1 yard (1 m) of brown ribbon. Wrap it around the edge of the board and secure with strips of double-sided tape. Leave the covered board out over night to allow it to dry.

2. Spoon 8 tablespoons of vanilla cake batter into a bowl and mix in the orange coloring. Add 12 tablespoons of vanilla batter to another bowl and mix in the cocoa powder.

3. Spoon the orange batter into a disposable pastry bag, twist and close. Repeat this with the brown batter. Line two 8-inch (20-cm) round sandwich cake pans with parchment paper.

4. Pour one-third of the uncolored vanilla cake batter into one of the prepared pans. Snip off the end of the pastry bag containing the brown batter and pipe 2 brown rings onto the uncolored vanilla batter—a small ring in the center and a larger ring outside it. You want the rings to be about 1 inch (2.5 cm) thick, with approximately 1 inch (2.5 cm) of the vanilla batter showing in between each ring and around the outer edge of the large ring.

4a.   4b.

5. Snip off the end of the pastry bag with the orange batter, ensuring the hole is smaller than that in the brown bag. Pipe orange rings on top of the brown. You should be able to see the brown around the edge of the orange. Take the pastry bag with the brown batter and pipe over the top of the orange rings, covering them completely.

6. Fill a third disposable pastry bag with the some vanilla batter and close. Snip off the tip and pipe the batter in the gaps between the rings and over them, covering them completely. Ensure you don't move the rings out of place as you work. Repeat steps 4, 5, and 6 with the second prepared cake pan.

7. Bake on the middle shelf of your oven for 50 minutes or until a cake tester comes out dry. Allow to cool in the pans for 10 minutes, then turn out onto a wire rack and leave to cool completely. Once cooled, turn the cake right side up (the part that was facing into the pan during baking is the bottom, and the uneven side is the top).

8. While the cakes are baking, prepare the leopard print decorations. Dust your work surface with confectioner's sugar, then roll the pale brown gumpaste into a long sausage. Repeat this with the dark brown gumpaste, then roll this out flat with a rolling pin. Using a dampened paintbrush, dampen the dark brown gumpaste and place the pale brown sausage shape on top. Wrap the dark brown flattened paste around the pale brown sausage shape to enclose it. Slice this into large ¼-inch (5-mm) slices and lay each slice flat. Roll out each slice to a thickness of ⅛ inch (3 mm).

9. Level the tops of your cakes if necessary (see pages 18–19). Put a small amount of buttercream onto the center of your prepared cake board. Position a cake layer centrally on the board and apply a thin layer of buttercream to the top of the layer. Align the second cake layer on top. Crumb coat the cake (see page 20) with buttercream and refrigerate for 30 minutes. Dust your work surface with confectioner's sugar, then roll out the orange fondant. Remove the cake from the refrigerator and cover the cake with the orange fondant (see page 22). Use a smoother and your hands to smooth the top, sides and edges of the cake.

10. To finish, use a dampened paintbrush to apply the leopard print decorations to the top and sides of the cake.

5.

6a.

6b.

8a.

8b.

8c.

Cloud Cake

Bring some color to a cloudy day with these billowy delights. No one will expect the rainbow within these cloud-shaped cakes and the revealing moment is sure to brighten up a dull day.

Preparation Time: 1 hour 15 minutes plus overnight drying, baking, and cooling | **Servings:** 6

1 lb 2 oz (500 g) blue ready-to-use fondant

Confectioner's sugar, to dust

1 x large batch Classic Vanilla Cake batter (see page 11)

Gel food colors in red, orange, yellow, green, blue, and purple

¼ x batch White Chocolate Ganache (see page 17)

14 oz (400 g) white ready-to-use fondant

1. Use the blue fondant to cover a 10-inch (25cm) square cake board (see page 21). You'll need roughly 1 yard (1 m) of blue ribbon. Wrap it around the edge of the board and secure it with strips of double-sided tape. Leave the fondant-covered board out overnight to allow it to dry.

2. Preheat the oven to 325ºF (160ºC). Line an 8-inch (20-cm) square cake pan with parchment paper. Divide the batter into 6 equal portions in separate bowls. Mix a different food coloring into each portion. Spoon the red mixture into the prepared cake pan so that it covers the bottom of the pan. Next, take the orange batter and spoon a layer on top of the red. Spoon a yellow layer on top of the orange. Repeat this process with the green batter, the blue and, finally, the purple-colored batter. Bake for 1 hour and 10 minutes or until a cake tester comes out clean. Allow to cool in the pan for 10 minutes, then turn out onto a wire rack and allow to cool completely. Note that the red side will be the top of your cake.

3. Once the cake has cooled, lay the cloud-shaped template (see page 138) flat on top of the cake and cut out the cloud shape (or cut it out freehand if you feel confident). Use a paring knife to carve the curved edges of your cloud. Now apply a small amount of white chocolate ganache to the center of your prepared cake board, then carefully pick up the cloud-shaped cake and stand it upright on the board. The ganache will stick the cake to the board. Crumb coat your cake with the ganache (see page 20) and refrigerate for 10 minutes to set.

4. Once set, cover the cake with the white fondant (see page 22). Use your hands to smooth the fondant over the edges, sides, and top of the cake. You may like to use any left over cake and create a smaller cloud.

Elegant Cakes

Neapolitan Cake 84

Ombre Cake 86

Hidden Cookie Cake 90

Ice Cream Cake 92

Neapolitan Cake

This classic combination of chocolate, strawberry, and vanilla flavors is always a winner, and saves you having to choose a flavor—everyone's favorite is bound to be in there, in each and every slice.

Preparation Time: 45 minutes plus baking, and cooling | **Servings:** 8–10

½ cup (2½ oz/70 g) superfine sugar

5 tbsp water

5½ oz (150 g) strawberries, hulled and quartered

1 x large batch Classic Vanilla Cake batter (see page 11)

¼ cup (¾ oz/20 g) unsweetened cocoa powder

½ tsp vanilla extract

2 x batches Classic Buttercream (see page 15)

1. Preheat the oven to 325ºF (160ºC). Line three 8-inch (20-cm) round sandwich cake pans with parchment paper. Make a strawberry coulis. Mix the superfine sugar into the water in a small saucepan and bring to a boil. Add the strawberries and cook for 2–3 minutes until they are soft. Remove from the heat and process the mixture with a hand-held blender until smooth. Allow the coulis to cool completely.

2. Divide the cake batter into 3 equal portions in separate bowls. Mix 2 tbsp strawberry coulis into 1 portion, the cocoa powder into another, and the vanilla extract into the final portion. Pour each portion into a separate cake pan and place in the oven. If you can fit in all three pans, great, but If you can't, bake 2, then bake the third separately. Bake for 30 minutes or until a cake tester comes out clean. Cool in the pans for 10 minutes, then turn out onto a wire rack and leave to cool completely.

3. If necessary, level the tops of the cake layers (see pages 18–19). Place a blob of buttercream onto the center of a 10-inch (25-cm) cake plate. Position the chocolate layer centrally on the plate and spread a layer of vanilla buttercream on top. Align the vanilla cake layer on top and press down firmly to stick the cake layers together. Spread over a layer of buttercream, then align the strawberry cake layer on the top, pressing down to stick the cake layers together. Crumb coat the cake (see page 20) with buttercream and refrigerate for 30 minutes to set.

4. Meanwhile, prepare a pastry bag (see page 24), fitting it with a star piping tip (Wilton 1M). Fill it with the remaining buttercream. Pipe roses onto the cake (see page 25), starting at the top center and working your way outward and down the sides. Refrigerate for 30 minutes to allow the frosting to set completely.

Ombre Cake

The exterior of this cake is elegant in its ruffled finery, while inside, the cake layers show a graduating range of shades that's very pleasing to the eye. Of course, you can use shades of any color you like to make this pretty cake that's perfect for a dinner party.

Preparation Time: 1 hour 45 minutes plus overnight drying, baking, and cooling | **Servings:** 15–20

3 lb (1.3 kg) white ready-to-use fondant
Confectioner's sugar
2 x large batches White Cake batter (see page 13)
Purple gel food coloring
White liquid food coloring
1 x batch Classic Buttercream (see page 15)
14 oz (400 g) white gumpaste

1. You'll need a 10-inch (25-cm) round cake board and 1 yard (1 m) purple ribbon for this project. Cover the cake board with white fondant (see page 21), then wrap the ribbon around the edge of the board and secure it with strips of double-sided tape. Leave the covered board out overnight to allow the fondant to dry.

2. Preheat the oven to 325ºF (160ºC). Pour the cake batter into a large bowl and add the purple gel food coloring until you achieve a dark purple shade. Divide the colored batter equally into 6 bowls. Set aside one bowl—this will be your darkest purple shade. Mix 1 tsp liquid white food coloring into the batter in the next bowl, 2 tsp into the next, and so on, until you have 6 shades of purple batter.

3. Line three 8-inch (20-cm) round cake pans with baking paper. Pour 1 shade of cake batter into each prepared pan and place in the oven. If you can fit all 3, great, but if not, bake in batches. Bake for 30 minutes or until a cake tester comes out clean. Turn the cakes out of the pans immediately onto a wire rack and leave to cool completely. Repeat this process with the remaining portions of cake batter. Once cooled, level off the tops of all the cakes (see pages 18–19).

4. Place a small blob of buttercream on the center of the prepared cake board and place the cake layer of the palest shade of purple on the center of the board. Spread over a layer of buttercream using an angled metal spatula, smoothing toward the edge and keeping it level. Align the cake layer of the second palest shade of purple on top and push down gently to secure it in place. Spread over buttercream as before, then position the cake layer of the next shade of purple on top. Continue in this way until you have stacked all the cake layers in

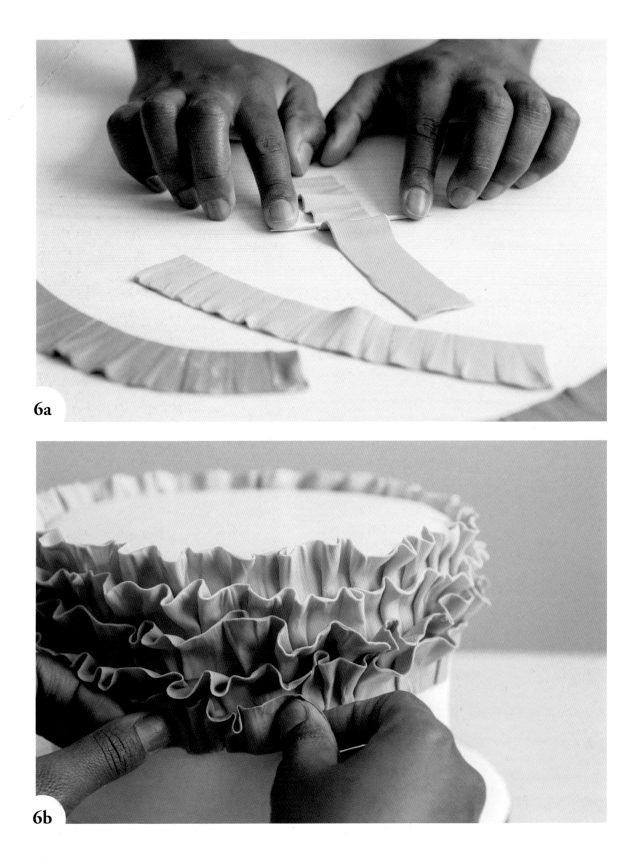

6a

6b

a graduating range of shades from palest purple at the bottom up to darkest purple at the top. Press down gently on the top of the stack to ensure the cake is level. Now crumb coat the cake (see page 20) with buttercream, then refrigerate for 30 minutes until set.

5. Cover the cake with the white fondant (see page 22). Allow the covered cake to sit for 1 hour.

6. Cut the gumpaste into 4 equal pieces. Use the gel food coloring to color each piece a different shade of purple, from pale to dark. Take the palest shade and roll out a strip that is roughly 1 inch (2.5 cm) wide and 5 inches (13 cm) long. Roll a toothpick across the strip, applying pressure to only 1 side of the strip to create a ruffled effect along that edge. Using a damp paintbrush, apply this strip, with the ruffled edge pointing up, to side of the cake so that it overlaps the top by roughly 1 inch (2.5 cm). As you apply the strip, gently gather it together a little to enhance the ruffled effect. When you need to join a new strip, overlap the beginning with the end of the previous strip. When you've completed the first ruffled layer, add another layer using a ruffled strip of the palest purple gumpaste. Work down the cake in this way with the remaining shades, using increasingly darker shades, applying 2 layers of each shade, until you have reached the bottom of the cake.

Hidden Cookie Cake

My brother André loves a good chocolate cake and this one is special as it is full of chocolate cookies—in the cake and in the filling! If you have any cookies left over, you can arrange them on top of the cake to hint at what's inside.

Preparation Time: 1 hour plus baking and cooling | **Servings:** 8–10

Approximately 14 Oreo cookies

1 × large batch Chocolate Cake batter (see page 14)

½ × batch Classic Buttercream (see page 15)

½ × batch Dark Chocolate Ganache (see page 17)

1. Preheat the oven to 325ºF (160ºC). Line two 8-inch (20-cm) sandwich cake pans with parchment paper.

2. Place 5–6 cookies in the bottom of each pan, spacing them out evenly. Divide the cake batter into 2 equal portions and pour a portion into each of the prepared pans. Bake for 40 minutes or until a cake tester comes out clean. Leave to cool in the pans for 10 minutes, then turn out onto a wire rack and allow to cool completely. Level off the tops of the cake layers (see pages 18–19).

3. Crumble the remaining cookies into large crumbs and place these in a bowl. Add the buttercream and mix thoroughly. Place a small blob of ganache on the center of a 10-inch (25-cm) serving plate. Position one cake layer on the plate and apply a generous amount of the buttercream-and-cookie-crumbs filling. Place the second cake layer firmly on top. Once stacked, crumb coat the cake (see page 20) with the ganache and refrigerate for 10 minutes to set.

4. To finish, cover the cake generously with a layer of ganache, using a dough scraper to create a smooth finish or, alternatively, creating a textured or stucco effect (see page 23) as shown on the cake in the picture opposite.

Ice Cream Cake

Having a summer party? Then why not try a surprise ice cream filling for the cake? You can choose any flavor of ice cream for this project, so go for your favorite. Serve the cake as soon as it is made for the best results.

Preparation Time: 1 hour plus baking and freezing | **Servings:** 8–10

7–8 scoops ice cream
1 × 8-inch (20-cm) round Classic Vanilla Cake (see page 11), leveled and cut into 2 equal layers
1 × batch Classic Buttercream (see page 15)

1. Take your ice cream out of the freezer and leave it out for 10 minutes to allow it to soften. Then stir it well to ensure that it has an even consistency.

2. Line an 8-inch (20-cm) round cake pan with a generous amount of plastic wrap. Make sure that you use enough plastic wrap to allow it to hang over the top edges of the pan and extend down the outside. Place 1 cake layer into the pan and press firmly to ensure it has reached the bottom of the pan.

3. Spoon 7–8 scoops of ice-cream into the pan on top of the cake layer and use an angled metal spatula to spread the ice cream evenly across the cake layer.

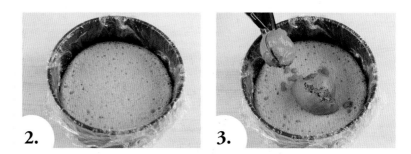

2.   3.

4. Place the second cake layer on top of the ice cream and press it firmly into the pan. Your cake will be slightly taller than the cake pan—this is fine, as long as at least half of the top layer is within the pan. Wrap up the cake with the overhanging plastic wrap, using additional plastic wrap if necessary to make sure the cake is completely covered. Place your cake pan in the freezer and leave it there for 1 hour in order to allow the ice-cream inside the cake to harden.

5. Take the cake out of the freezer, transfer it to a plate, and apply a crumb coat (see page 20) using the vanilla buttercream. Now place the cake back into the freezer and leave it in there for 10 minutes to allow the crumb coat to set.

6. Remove from the freezer and coat with a generous layer of buttercream. Place the cake on a 10-inch (25-cm) cake plate and serve immediately.

TIP

If you need to delay serving, the finished cake can be wrapped in plastic wrap and stored in the freezer until you are ready to serve. Allow it to sit at room temperature for 5–10 minutes before serving.

4.

5a.

5b.

6.

Holidays and Special Occasions

Gender Surprise Cake

Using a cake to tell your family and friends if you're having a baby boy or girl has become a popular way to share the news. The sponge is colored either pink or blue, then hidden by a tempting layer of frosting. At the baby shower or gathering thrown to celebrate the pregnancy, the cake is cut and the gender is revealed in a fun and exciting way. The hidden checkerboard pattern adds visual appeal.

Preparation Time: 1 hour plus baking and cooling | **Servings:** 8–10

1 x large and 1 x small batch White Cake batter (see page 13)
Food gel color in pink or blue
1 × batch White Chocolate Ganache (see page 17)

1. Preheat the oven to 325°F (160°C). Line four 8-inch (20-cm) round sandwich pans with parchment paper.

2. Divide the batter equally into 2 separate bowls. Mix some gel food coloring into each bowl, adding more to one bowl than to the other to give you 2 shades of either pink or blue. Spoon the mixtures into the prepared pans so that you have 2 pans containing the paler shade of your chosen color and 2 containing the darker shade.

3. Place 2 of the pans in the oven and bake for 30 minutes or until a cake tester comes out clean. Turn out onto a wire rack and allow to cool. Repeat with the remaining 2 pans of batter so you have 2 cake layers of each shade of either pink or blue.

4. If necessary, level off the tops of your cake layers (see pages 18–19) and cut off any brown areas of sponge on the surfaces of the layers (make sure you do this without reshaping the layers). You'll now need two round cutters, one with a diameter of 4½ inches (12 cm) and the other, 3¼ inches (8 cm). Place one of the cake layers on your work surface and position the round cutters in concentric circles on the top surface of the layer, ensuring they are both centered. Carefully press down to cut out 3 rings (*see picture on page 100*). Repeat this process with the remaining 3 cake layers. You now have 2 large and 2 medium-sized rings and 2 small circles of each shade of your chosen color—so 4 large rings, 4 medium-sized rings, and 4 small circles in total.

❧ Holidays and Special Occasions ❧

5. Now it's time to assemble the cake. Smear a small amount of ganache onto the center of a 10-inch (25-cm) cake plate. Take 1 of the large rings of your darker shade and position this on the cake plate. Inside this, place a medium-sized ring of the paler shade. Inside this, place a small circle of the darker shade. You've now assembled the first cake layer. Spread over a thin layer of ganache. Now assemble the second layer. Align a large ring of the paler shade with the first layer. Inside this, place a medium-sized ring of the darker shade. Inside this, place a small circle of the paler shade. Once again, spread over a thin layer of ganache. You now have 2 cake layers of alternating shades of concentric circles. Repeat the process with the remaining cake shapes to complete assembling the layers. Once assembled, press down on the stack to stick the layers together.

6. Crumb coat the cake (see page 20) with some of the remaining ganache and refrigerate for 10 minutes. Once the crumb coat has set, apply a generous layer of ganache using a spatula, ensuring you cover up all traces of your chosen color.

4.

5.

New Year's Countdown Cake

Add some glamour to your New Year's celebrations with this fabulous party cake, in which each slice reveals a number from 10 to 1. Sharing this glitzy confection with friends is certainly a stylish way to count in the new year.

Preparation Time: 1 hour 45 minutes plus overnight drying, baking, and freezing | **Servings:** 10

3 lb (1.3 kg) black ready-to-use fondant
Confectioner's sugar, to dust
1¾ oz (50 g) yellow gumpaste
Edible gold paint
2 × Chocolate Cakes baked in loaf pans (see page 14)
1 × large batch Classic Vanilla Cake batter (see page 11)
1 × batch Dark Chocolate Ganache (see page 17)
Edible gold glitter

1. Cover a 10-inch (25-cm) round cake board with black fondant (see page 21). You'll need 1 yard (1 m) of black ribbon. Wrap it around the edge of the board and secure it with strips of double-sided tape. Leave the covered board out overnight to allow the fondant to dry.

2. Roll out the yellow gumpaste to a thickness of roughly ¹⁄₁₆ inch (2 mm). You'll need a set of number-shaped cookie cutters to cut out numbers to decorate the top of your cake (for the top of the cake in the picture on page 102, stylized sugarcraft cutters were used). Use cutters for the numbers 12, 3, 6, and 9. Also, cut out both a long and short hand for your clock, using the picture on page 102 to guide you for shape, and the bottom of an 8-inch (20-cm) round cake pan to help you estimate how long they should be. Cut a small circle to cover the spot where the two clock hands will be joined. Place the yellow gumpaste numbers, clock hands, and circle on a sheet of parchment paper and use a paintbrush to cover them in edible gold paint. Set aside to dry overnight.

3. Slice each of your chocolate loaf cakes into 10 equal slices, each with a thickness of approximately 1 inch (2.5 cm). Using number cutters, cut out the numbers 1 to 10 from the slices of cake so that you have 3 of each number. One slice of chocolate loaf cake will yield 3–4 number shapes, depending on the size of cutters used. Once cut, place the numbers on a sheet of parchment paper set on a baking sheet and cover with plastic wrap, then freeze for 2 hours or until frozen.

4. Preheat the oven to 325°F (160°C). Line an 8-inch (20-cm) round cake pan with parchment paper. Remove the numbers from the freezer. Pour enough of the vanilla cake batter into the prepared pan to coat

the bottom. Now position your countdown numbers. First, decide where the 'top' of the cake should be (this will correspond with 12 o'clock), then begin to assemble the cut-out numbers in the pan. Position 2–3 pieces of the number 1 at the top of the circle, placing them upright into the cake batter, back to back, about 1 inch (2.5 cm) in from the sides of the pan. Working counter-clockwise around the pan, continue to add the cut-out numbers into the pan, adding number 2, then 3, and so on all the way to number 10, bringing you right around the perimeter of the pan and back to the number one. Once all the numbers are in place, push a bamboo skewer into the batter where the number 1 is positioned, to mark the 'top' of your countdown. Spoon the rest of your cake batter into a disposable pastry bag and snip off the end. Pipe the batter around and over the numbers, making sure you don't move any of them out of place.

5. Bake on the middle shelf of the oven for 1 hour and 10 minutes, or until a cake tester comes out dry. Allow to cool in the pan for 10 minutes, then turn out onto a wire rack and allow to cool completely, removing the toothpick from the top of the cake and replacing it on the bottom of the cake to mark where the top of your countdown is.

6. Once cooled, turn the cake right-side up, remarking the top of your countdown with the toothpick. Put a small amount of ganache onto the center of your prepared cake board. Place the cake on the center of the board. Crumb coat your cake (see page 20) with dark chocolate ganache and refrigerate for 10 minutes to set.

7. Remove the toothpick from the cake (but ensure you know where the number 1 is inside your cake is. Roll out the remaining black fondant to a thickness of ¼ inch (5 mm). Cover the cake with the fondant (see page 22).

8. Stick the gold-painted numbers onto the cake using a dampened paintbrush, placing number 12 at the 'top' of the cake, number 6 at the bottom, number 3 on the right, and number 9 on the left, as per a clock face. Place the hands of the clock showing 11:50 pm and cover the join with the gold-painted circle. Sprinkle some gold glitter onto the cake board around the sides of the cake and on top of each number.

Independence Day Cake

Cake shapes lend themselves very well to depicting the colors and broad shapes of the American flag, so what better way to celebrate Independence Day than with this cheerful confectionary homage to the good old stars and stripes?

Preparation Time: 1 hour 30 minutes plus overnight drying, baking, and cooling | **Servings:** 8–10

1 lb 2 oz (500g) white ready-to-use fondant
2 × large batches White Cake batter (see page 13)
Gel food colors in red and blue
1 × batch Classic Buttercream (see page 15)

1. Cover a 10-inch (25-cm) round cake board with the white fondant (see page 21). You'll need 1 yard (1 m) of red ribbon for this project. Wrap the ribbon around the edge of the board and secure it with strips of double-sided tape. Leave the covered cake board out overnight to allow the fondant to dry.

2. Preheat the oven to 325°F (160°C). Divide the cake batter into 3 equal portions and spoon each portion into a separate bowl. Using the gel food colors, color one portion red and another portion blue, mixing the colors through the batter thoroughly with a tablespoon. Leave the remaining portion uncolored.

3. Line three 8-inch (20-cm) round sandwich cake pans with parchment paper. You'll need to have 2 red layers, 2 blue layers, and 2 white layers in total, so divide each bowl of batter into 2 equal portions. Pour 3 of these portions into the prepared cake pans and place them in the oven. If you can fit all 3, great, but if you can't, bake the portions in batches). Bake for 30 minutes or until a cake tester comes out clean. Cool in the pans for 10 minutes, then turn out the cakes onto a wire rack and allow to cool completely. Repeat with the remaining portions of batter. Once cooled, level the tops of all 6 cakes using a cake leveler (see pages 18–19).

4. Take 2 blue layers, 1 red layer, and 1 white layer. Using a 6-inch (15-cm) round cookie cutter, remove the center from each of these 4 cake layers. You will need to use the outer ring of both blue layers, and the centre circle of the red and white layers. Discard the remaining cut pieces of cake.

5. Apply a little buttercream to the center of your presentation board. Place the uncut red layer on the center of the board. Spread over a thin layer of buttercream using an angled metal spatula, smoothing the filling toward the edges and keeping it level. Align the uncut white layer on top and push down to secure it in place. Spread over some buttercream, then align a blue ring on top, then insert the red circle of cake into its center. Push down on these 2 pieces until they are level with one another. Now spread over some buttercream and align the final blue ring on top, then position the white cake circle in its center.

6. Crumb coat the cake (see page 20) with some more buttercream and refrigerate for 30 minutes to set. Once set, apply a final layer of buttercream.

4.

5.

Lucky Clover Cake

*Say Happy St Patrick's Day with this cheeky, eye-catching dessert that mimics a leprechaun's hat.
The best thing about this cake is that everyone receives a lucky four-leaf clover!*

Preparation Time: 1 hour 30 minutes plus overnight drying, baking, and freezing | **Servings:** 10

**3 lb (1.3 kg) green ready-to-use
fondant**
Confectioner's sugar, to dust
**2 × Classic Vanilla Cakes baked
in loaf pans (see page 11),
colored green**
**1 × large batch Classic Vanilla
Cake batter (see page 11)**
**1 × batch Dark Chocolate
Ganache (see page 17)**
3½ oz(100 g) black gumpaste
1¾ oz (50 g) yellow gumpaste

1. Cover a 10-inch (25-cm) round cake board with green fondant (see page 21). This will be the base of your hat. You'll need 1 yard (1 m) of green ribbon. Wrap it around the edge of the board and secure it with strips of double-sided tape. Leave the covered board out overnight to allow the fondant to dry.

2. Slice each of your green vanilla loaf cakes into 10 equal slices, each with a thickness of approximately 1 inch (2.5 cm).

3. Using the template on page 139 or a clover-shaped cookie cutter, cut out 12–14 clovers. Lay them on a baking sheet lined with parchment paper and cover with plastic wrap. Freeze for 2 hours.

4. Preheat the oven to 325°F (160°C). Line an 8-inch (20-cm) round cake pan with parchment paper. Prepare the vanilla cake batter.

5. Remove the clover shapes from the freezer. Pour enough cake batter into the prepared pan to coat the bottom. Place some of the clovers into the mixture roughly 1 inch (2.5 cm) from the sides of the pan until you have formed a ring. The clovers meet at the inner part of the ring, but there are gaps along the outer edges of the ring. Use the remaining clovers to make wedge-shaped clovers to fill these gaps. To do this, stand a remaining clover shape upright on your work surface. Slice this in half vertically, but instead of slicing it into 2 equal halves to create thinner slices, place the knife diagonally across the top plane and slice down to create 2 wedges (*see picture on page 109*). These have a clover shape when viewed from the sides, but are wedge-shaped when viewed from above. Slide these wedges into position between the clover shapes in the pan to fill the gaps (*see picture on page 109*).

6. Fill a disposable pastry bag with the remaining batter and close. Snip off the tip and pipe the batter around and over the ring of clovers, ensuring you don't move any of the shapes out of position. Bake on the middle shelf of your oven for 1 hour and 10 minutes or until a cake tester comes out dry. Allow to cool in the pan for 10 minutes, then turn out onto a wire rack and allow to cool completely. Once cooled, turn the cake right-side up.

7. Put a small amount of ganache onto the center of your prepared cake board. Place the cake onto the board and apply a crumb coat (see page 18) with dark chocolate ganache. Refrigerate for 10 minutes. Roll out the remaining green fondant and use it to cover the cake (see page 22).

8. Now prepare the hat belt. Roll out a long strip of black gumpaste to a thickness of roughly ⅛ inch (3 mm). Cut a rectangular strip that's about 1½ inches (4 cm) wide and 25 inches (65 cm) long. Using a dampened paintbrush, stick this strip to the bottom edge of the cake. Use a paring knife to trim away any excess gumpaste at the join. Roll out the yellow gumpaste. Cut out a rectangle that has the same width as the hat belt. Now cut out and discard the center of this rectangle to leave a ¼ inch (5 mm) rectangular border. This will be the buckle. Use a dampened paintbrush to stick this onto the hat belt.

5a. 5b.

Christmas Tree Cake

Surprise family and friends with this wonderfully festive reveal—a vivid green Christmas tree baked into a delicious chocolate cake! From the first slice to the last, you'll enjoy this visual delight.

Preparation Time: 1 hour plus baking and cooling | **Servings:** 15–18

1 × 8-inch (20-cm) round **Classic Vanilla Cake (see page 11), colored green**

1 heaped tablespoon **Classic Buttercream (see page 15)**

3 × 6-inch (15-cm) round **Chocolate Cake layers, each 2–3 inches (5–7.5 cm) tall (see page 12—use 1 x large batch of batter), leveled**

½ × batch **Dark Chocolate Ganache (see page 17)**

1. Break the green cake into crumbs by hand into a bowl. Mix in the buttercream. Set aside.

2. For this project, you'll need both a 3-inch (7.5-cm) and a 2-inch (5-cm) round cookie cutter. Place 1 chocolate cake layer on your work surface. Insert the 2-inch (5-cm) round cookie cutter at the center of the top of the cake layer and push it all the way through the cake to the bottom. Leave the smaller cutter inserted in the cake. Now position your 3-inch (7.5-cm) cutter on the center of the top of the cake, around the smaller cutter, and use it to score the surface of the cake. Remove the cutter.

3. Now it is time to cut out the center of the cake layer. Insert a paring knife into the cake at an angle somewhere along your score mark, ensuring the tip of the knife comes into contact with the bottom of the smaller cutter. Using the score mark as a guide, slowly cut out the centre of the cake, keeping the tip of the knife in contact with the bottom of the cutter. Remove the inserted cutter and discard the center of the cake. You now have a circular hole with sloped sides that has a diameter of 3 inches (7.5 cm) on one side of the cake layer and 2 inches (5 cm) on the other side. Repeat this step with another layer of chocolate cake. These 2 cakes will be the lower 2 layers of your finished cake.

4. Place the remaining cake layer on your work surface. Push a toothpick into the center of the cake and insert it all the way through the cake. Use the 3-inch (7.5-cm) round cookie cutter to score a circle at the center of the top of this cake layer. Now insert the paring knife at an angle somewhere along your score mark, ensuring the tip of the

knife comes into the contact with the bottom of the toothpick. Using the score line as a guide, slowly cut a cone shape out of the center of the cake, keeping the tip of the knife in contact with the toothpick as you move the knife. Remove and discard this cut-out piece. This layer will be the top layer of your cake.

5. Place the lower 2 cake layers on the work surface with the 3-inch (7.5-cm) circle facing upward. Insert a toothpick into the top cake layer so you can identify it later. Spoon the green cake crumb-and-buttercream mixture into the recesses you cut, filling each one to the top of the recess. Press down on the filling with the back of your spoon to compact it and ensure that each recess is completely filled. Note that the side of each layer that you are filling the recesses from (with the larger cut-out circle) is the bottom of the layer.

6. Apply a thin layer of ganache to the bottom of one of the lower cake layers around the recess, ensuring the ganache does not touch the green filling. Carefully and quickly turn this over and place it onto an 8-inch (20-cm) cake plate. Spread a thin layer of ganache on the other lower cake layer in the same way and stack it on top of the bottom layer. Remove the toothpick from the top cake layer and spread a thin layer of ganache on the bottom of the layer. Align this on top of the first 2 layers. Push down on the top of the stack to ensure the layers are well adhered to one another.

7. Crumb coat the sides and the top of the cake (see page 20) with some of the ganache. Refrigerate for 10 minutes to set.

8. To finish, add another generous layer of ganache to the cake, using a dough scraper for a smooth finish.

4.

5.

Easter Egg Minicakes

A cake inside an egg?! That's right, a cake baked inside an egg shell. This one never fails to surprise people! No one will believe you until they crack it open to see for themselves. Give a box of these cute little treats to friends and family for a special Easter gift.

Preparation Time: 1 hour plus drying, baking, and cooling | **Servings:** 12

12 eggs (keep the boxes for packaging)
1 × small batch Classic Vanilla Cake batter (see page 11)
Gel food colors of your choice (optional)

1. Gently tap a hole into the bottom of an egg using a cake tester or pin. Once cracked, peel away some of the eggshell around the hole to enlarge the hole a little. It should be just large enough for a round piping tip (Wilton 1A) to fit into it.

2. Gently shake the egg over a bowl so that the contents emerge through the hole. You may need to use your cake tester or a toothpick to get the yolk to burst, which makes it easier to get it out of the eggshell. Discard the contents, or pop them into a container and store in the fridge to use in another recipe. Repeat steps 1 and 2 with the remaining eggs.

3. Once the shells are empty, carefully rinse them inside and out under cold running water, then soak them in a bowl of warm salt water for 1 hour (*see picture on page 114*). This will remove any excess egg.

4. Empty the water out of the eggshells and rinse them under cold running water once more. Set the shells on some paper towels to dry.

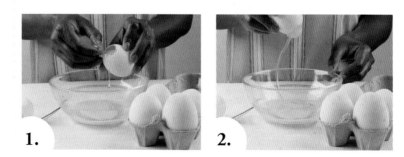

1.　**2.**

3.

5. While the eggshells are drying, prepare your cake batter. If you are coloring the batter, allow for 3 tbsp of batter per egg.

6. Preheat the oven to 325ºF (160ºC). Place a 12-cup silicone cupcake pan on a baking sheet. Make 12 small aluminum foil nests, one for each recess in the cupcake pan. Rest each eggshell, with the hole facing upward, in one of these foil nests in the cupcake pan.

7. Prepare a pastry bag (see page 24), fitting it with the piping tip. (Note that you'll need one pastry bag and piping tip for each color of batter you are using.) Pipe the batter into each eggshell until it is two-thirds full. Bake for 20 minutes or until a cake tester comes out clean. Allow the eggs to cool in the cupcake pan until completely cool.

8. Using a paring knife, trim away any excess cake around the edges of the hole in each eggshell and use a damp paper towel to rub away any excess cake crumbs. To finish, place the eggs back into their original box with the hole facing downward. The lucky recipient of this special Easter gift will be none-the-wiser until they try to crack one open!

7.

8.

Advanced Cakes

◆

Secret Garden Cake

*Shhh! Don't let on to your guests that this gorgeous cake is not just pretty on the outside.
There is a secret garden hidden within it.*

Preparation Time: 1 hour 45 minutes plus overnight drying, baking, and freezing | **Servings:** 8–10

3 lb (1.3 kg) green ready-to-use fondant

Confectioner's sugar, to dust

2 × Classic Vanilla Cakes baked in loaf pans (see page 11), colored pink

1 × Classic Vanilla Cake baked in a loaf pan (see page 11), colored yellow

1 × large batch Classic Vanilla Cake batter (see page 11), colored green

7 oz (200 g) white gumpaste

Gel food colors in pink, purple, yellow, and orange

1 × batch White Chocolate Ganache (see page 17)

1. You'll need a 10-inch (25-cm) round cake board and 1 yard (1 m) green ribbon for this project. Cover the cake board with green fondant. Wrap the ribbon around the edge of the board and secure it with strips of double-sided tape. Leave the fondant-covered board out overnight to allow the fondant to dry.

2. Slice each of your pink and yellow vanilla loaf cakes into 10 equal slices, each with a thickness of approximately 1 inch (2.5 cm). Using the flower template on page 139 or a large flower-shaped cutter, cut out a flower shape from each pink slice until you have 16–20 flowers. Now, using a ¾-inch (2-cm) circular cookie cutter, remove the centers of the pink flower-shaped cake pieces (discard these centers). Now use the same circular cutter to cut out 16–20 circles from the yellow cake slices. Place a yellow circle in the center of each pink flower. Place the finished flowers on a piece of parchment paper set on a baking sheet and cover with plastic wrap. Freeze for 2 hours or until frozen.

3. Preheat the oven to 325ºF (160ºC). Line an 8-inch (20-cm) round cake pan with parchment paper.

4. Remove the flower shapes from the freezer. Pour enough of the vanilla cake batter into the prepared pan to coat the bottom of the pan. Place some of the flowers inside the mixture roughly 1 inch (2.5 cm) from the sides of the pan until you have formed a ring *(see picture 5a on page 109, which shows this technique with clover-shaped piece of cake).* The flowers will meet at the inner part of the ring, but there are gaps along the outer edges of the ring between the flowers. You now need to use the remaining flower shapes to make wedge-shaped flowers to fill these gaps. To do this, stand a remaining flower shape upright on your

work surface. Slice this in half vertically, but instead of slicing it into 2 equal halves to create thinner slices, place the knife diagonally across the top plane and slice down to create 2 wedges *(see picture 5b on page 109, which shows this technique with clover-shaped piece of cake)*. These still have a flower shape when viewed from the side, but are wedge-shaped when viewed from above. Position these wedge-shaped flowers in between each of the flower shape that are in the pan. Once the flower shapes are aligned in the pan, fill a disposable pastry bag with the remaining batter and close. Snip off the tip and pipe the batter around and over the flowers, ensuring you don't move any of them out of place. Bake on the middle shelf of your oven for 50 minutes or until a cake tester comes out clean.

5. Meanwhile, cut the gumpaste into 4 equal pieces and color each piece with a different gel food color. Roll out one of the pieces on a work surface dusted with confectioner's sugar. Using flower-shaped cutters in a variety of sizes, cut out flower shapes to decorate the top and sides of the cake. Repeat with the remaining colored gumpaste. Leave the flower shapes out to dry.

6. Remove the cake from the oven and allow to cool in the pan for 10 minutes, then turn it out onto a wire rack and leave to cool completely.

7. Crumb coat the cake (see page 20) with white chocolate ganache and refrigerate for 10 minutes. Place a small amount of ganache on the center of your prepared cake board. Position the cake on the center of the board, ensuring the cake is the correct way up (you want the internal flower design to be toward the bottom of the cake). Roll out the remaining green fondant and use it to cover the cake (see page 22). Use a smoother and your hands to smooth the top, sides, and edges of the cake.

8. Arrange the gumpaste flowers on your cake and cake board as desired. Use a dampened paintbrush to stick the flowers to the cake.

Hidden Passion Minicakes

This is the perfect treat for a romantic dinner date. Red love hearts attached to the outer layer hint at what's inside, and once cut, your loved one won't be able to fathom how you achieved the vertical stripes! The pretty hearts are an addition inspired by my friend Davina.

Preparation Time: 45 minutes plus baking and chilling | **Servings:** 4

1¾ oz (50 g) red gumpaste

Confectioner's sugar, to dust

½ cup (4½ oz/125 g) unsalted butter, softened

¾ cup (5½ oz/150 g) superfine sugar

1 extra-large egg, at room temperature

1¼ cups (5 oz/140 g) all-purpose flour

1 tbsp unsweetened cocoa powder

½ tsp baking soda

Pinch of salt

½ cup (4½ fl oz/125 ml) buttermilk

1 tsp vanilla extract

1 tsp white wine vinegar

2 tsp red gel food coloring

2 tbsp water

½ × batch Classic Buttercream (see page 15)

1 lb 10 oz (750 g) white ready-to-use fondant

1. Preheat oven to 350°F (180°C). Line a jellyroll pan that's roughly 14 × 9 inches (35 × 23 cm) with parchment paper.

2. Roll out the red gumpaste on a work surface dusted with confectioner's sugar. Use a heart-shaped cutter that's roughly ½ inch (1 cm) tall and wide to cut out 20–25 hearts. Set aside.

3. Fit the paddle attachment to a stand mixer. Set the mixer to a medium speed, then blend together butter and superfine sugar until the mixture is pale. Add the egg and mix it in thoroughly. Stop the mixer and scrape down the sides of the bowl.

4. In a medium-sized bowl, sift together the flour, cocoa powder, baking soda, and salt.

5. In a small jug, mix together the buttermilk, vanilla extract, and white wine vinegar.

6. Add half of the dry ingredients to the butter, sugar, and egg mixture in the bowl of the stand mixer and blend on a low speed. Once incorporated, add half of the buttermilk mixture. Once incorporated, scrape down the sides of the bowl and repeat, adding the rest of your dry and liquid ingredients to the bowl in the same way.

7. In a small jug, stir the red gel food coloring into the water, ensuring the gel is completely dissolved and that there are no lumps. Pour this into your mixture and blend in the color on a slow speed until it is evenly distributed throughout.

8. Spoon the colored mixture into the prepared pan, ensuring it reaches the corners. Bake for 20 minutes, until the center of the sponge bounces back when touched.

9. Dampen a dish towel with cold water and place it on top of the cake. Flip over the pan (use a dry dish towel to handle the jellyroll pan as this will be hot). Gently and slowly peel away the parchment paper. Tightly roll up the cake up, starting the roll along one of the longest edges, in the damp dish towel, then leave for at least 30 minutes to allow it to cool completely.

10. Carefully unroll the cake—it will be very moist so do this slowly, to avoid tearing the sponge, but don't worry if it does tear, as the cake will still roll back into shape. Spread the buttercream across the top, starting from the middle and spreading outward until it reaches ½ inch (1 cm) from the edges. The cream should be approximately ¼ inch (5 mm) thick, which is roughly the same thickness as that of your cake. Now carefully reroll your cake.

11. Slice your swiss roll into 4 equal pieces. Sit these upright on a plate and refrigerate for 30 minutes. Using an angled metal spatula, apply a thin crumb coat (see page 20) to your cake and refrigerate for 30 minutes.

12. Roll out the white fondant to a thickness of ¼ inch (5 mm) on a work surface dusted with confectioner's sugar. Make sure the surface area is large enough to cut out 3 large circles with which to cover your cakes. Cut out 1 circle, then remove 1 cake from the refrigerator and cover it with the fondant (see page 22). Now set the cake in position on your presentation plate. Repeat with the remaining cakes.

13. Apply your hearts around the base of the cakes, using a dampened paintbrust to stick them in place. When serving, slice down the center of the cake for the best visual impact.

11a.

11b.

Bumblebee Cake

This cake is great for children's birthday parties and the stripy inside gives the design a lovely surprise element. The recipe yields enough for two cakes, so you can have a pair of bees at the party.

Preparation Time: 1 hour 45 minutes plus overnight drying, baking, and cooling | **Servings:** 6–8

1 lb 2 oz (500 g) green ready-to-use fondant

Confectioner's sugar, to dust

1 × large batch Classic Vanilla Cake batter (see page 11)

Gel food colors in yellow, black, pink, orange, and green

3½ oz (100 g) white gumpaste

½ × batch Classic Buttercream (see page 15)

1 lb 5 oz (600 g) yellow ready-to-use fondant

7 oz (200 g) black ready-to-use fondant

1. Cover a 10-inch (25-cm) round cake board with green fondant (see page 21). You'll need 1 yard (1 m) of green ribbon. Wrap it around the edge of the board and secure it with strips of double-sided tape. Now make the antennae. Roll 2 small balls of black fondant and insert a toothpick into each one about half way into the ball. Set aside. Take 2 toothpicks and insert them into a ball of spare fondant. Use a paintbrush to apply a thin layer of black gel food coloring to each toothpick until they are black. Leave the covered board and the antennae out overnight to allow the fondant to dry.

2. Divide the cake batter into 2 equal portions in separate bowls. Use gel food colors to color 1 portion yellow and the other black. Spray a dome-shaped cake pan or heatproof glass bowl that has a 6-inch (15-cm) diameter with cake-release spray. Pour a portion of cake batter into the pan or bowl, filling it two-thirds of the way up the sides. Bake on the middle shelf of the oven for 30 minutes or until a cake tester comes out clean. Allow to cool in the pan for 10 minutes, then turn out onto a wire rack and allow to cool completely. Repeat with the other portion of batter. (If you have two identical pans/bowls, bake both batches simultaneously.)

3. Meanwhile, cut your white gumpaste into 4 equal pieces. Color 1 piece pink, another yellow and a third, orange. Leave 1 portion white. Set aside half of the white portion. Roll out each color and use flower-shaped sugarcraft cutters to cut out flower shapes *(see picture on page 129)*. These will be arranged around the edges of your cake. Leave these out to allow them to dry.

4. Line up the 2 cakes, one behind the other. Slicing through the aligned cakes simultaneously, as shown in the picture opposite, cut each cake in half vertically, then slice each of the halves in half. Swap the corresponding pieces of each cake with one another and select one set to work with (or cover an additional cake board with fondant and prepare 2 cakes). Align the alternating pieces of colored cake, bringing them together in a dome shape with a striped yellow-and-black pattern.

5. Put a small amount of buttercream onto the center of your prepared cake board. Place the black center piece of your cake onto the board. Using a spatula, apply some buttercream to the cut sides of this portion of cake. Stick a yellow piece to the buttercream on either side of the black piece. One of these yellow pieces is an end piece, while the other has an exposed cut side. Finish by applying buttercream to this exposed side of the yellow piece and position the black end piece to complete the dome. Apply gentle but firm pressure to the sides to stick the vertical layers together. Pierce a toothpick into the center of the bottom edge of the black end piece (this will be the back of your cake). Crumb coat the cake (see page 20) with buttercream. Refrigerate for 30 minutes to set. Set aside the remaining buttercream.

6. Remove the cake from the refrigerator and take out the toothpick, ensuring you know which side is the back. Roll out the yellow fondant and cover the cake (see page 22). Replace the toothpick into its previous position to mark the back of the cake.

7. Roll out the reserved white gumpaste to a thickness of ⅛ inch (3 mm). Use a 2-inch (5-cm) round cookie cutter to cut out 2 circles. You'll use these to make the eyes. Use a dampened paintbrush to stick these to the front of the cake, using the picture on page 129 as a placement guide. Roll out 2 balls with the remaining black fondant and flatten them. Stick these to the white circles to make the pupils. Roll out a small ball of black fondant and create a point. Remove your toothpick and replace it with the black point, using a dampened paintbrush to stick it to the cake. Pierce the ends of the antennae toothpicks into the head of the bumblebee, using the picture on page 127 as a placement guide.

8. Roll out the black fondant to a thickness of ⅛ inch (3 mm). Slice three 1-inch (2.5-cm) thick black strips that are roughly 8 inches (20 cm) long. Use a dampened paintbrush to stick these across the

Advanced Cakes

3.

4a.

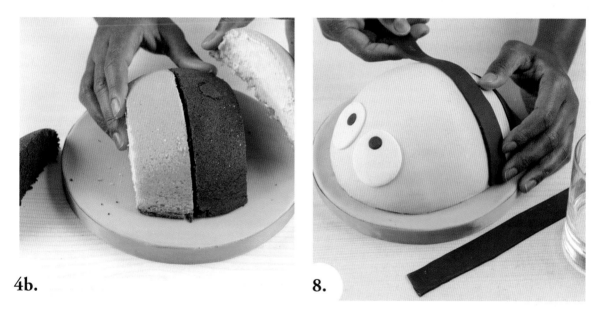

4b.

8.

top of the cake, from side to side—start with a strip across the middle, then add another strip on the other side of this center strip. Now use a paring knife to trim away any black fondant that overlaps the cake board.

9. Mix some green gel food coloring into the remaining buttercream. Prepare a pastry bag (see page 24) and fit it with a grass piping tip (Wilton 233). Fill it with the green buttercream and pipe grass onto the cake board around the edges of the cake. To finish, arrange the gumpaste flowers around the cake on top of the grass.

Candy Jar Cake

Making this project is a great way to say Happy Birthday to any candy lover! When making for a friend, choose their favorite candies and put their name on the front of the jar. If you are lucky, they may even share some with you!

Preparation Time: 45 minutes plus overnight drying, baking, and chilling | **Servings:** 12

3 lb (1.3 kg) ivory ready-to-use fondant

Confectioner's sugar, to dust

2 × 6-inch (15-cm) round Classic Vanilla Cakes (see page 11—use 1 x large batch of batter), each leveled and cut into 2 layers

1 × batch White Chocolate Ganache (see page 17)

5½ oz (150 g) candy bon bons

TIP

Choose any combination of candies and change the color of the jar to suit your party theme.

1. You need a 6-inch (15-cm) round cake board to make a lid for your jar and an 8-inch (20-cm) round cake board for presentation. Cover your cake boards with ivory fondant (see page 21). Use some of the remaining fondant to roll out 2 ping-pong ball sized spheres. Flatten 1 into a disk. Stick this onto the center of the smaller board using a dampened paintbrush. Stick the ball to the center of the disk to form a mock handle for the lid. You'll need 2 yards (2 m) of ribbon. Wrap it around each board and secure it with strips of double-sided tape. Leave the covered boards out overnight to allow to dry.

2. Use a 3-inch (7.5-cm) round cookie cutter to remove the center from 3 of the cake layers. Discard the centers to leave 3 cake rings and 1 intact cake layer. Apply a little ganache to the center of the presentation board and place the uncut cake layer on the center. Apply a layer of ganache on this layer, avoiding the area where the central well will be, then align a cake ring on top. Repeat this process until all 3 cake rings are stacked, ensuring they are aligned. Avoid applying ganache to the central well inside the rings. Crumb coat the cake (see page 20) with ganache and refrigerate for 10 minutes to set.

3. Roll out the remaining ivory fondant in a circle that's roughly 12 inches (30 cm) in diameter, with a thickness of ¼ inch (5 mm). Cover the cake with the fondant (see page 22). It will cover the hole in the top of your cake. Cut out a corresponding hole in the fondant with a paring knife. Smooth the cut edge near the inside of the top ring.

4. Pour your chosen candies into the central well and place the cake-board lid on top. To finish, pop a few candies on the side of the jar for decoration.

You're a Gem!

Brighten up someone's day with this multilayered cake that's designed to show how precious they are to you. I've chosen green for emerald for the cake shown here, but you can easily change the type of gemstone you portray by changing the food coloring—purple for amethyst, red for ruby, and so on.

Preparation Time: 1 hour plus baking and chilling | **Servings:** 15–18

5 × 6-inch (15-cm) square White Cakes (see page 13—use 5 x small batches of batter)
1 × batch Classic Buttercream (see page 15), colored white
Green gel food coloring in 3 shades

1. Use a cake leveler (see page 18) to cut off the tops of all of your cakes so that they are all 1 inch (2.5 cm) high and the tops are all level. Set aside the offcuts, trimming and discarding the brown parts. Put a small blob of frosting on the center of your cake presentation plate, then place a cake layer on top. Push it down to fix the cake in place. Align 2 more cake layers on top of this cake.

2. You'll need 2 copies of each of the 2 templates for this project on page 139. Take the 2 copies of the template labeled 'bottom'. Hold one against the center of one side of the top layer of the stack so that the edge marked A on the template is flush with the top edge of the cake. Use toothpicks to hold the template in position. Position the duplicate template in the corresponding spot on the opposite side of the top layer. Using the diagonal lines at the sides of the templates to guide you, use a long serrated knife to cut out the middle portions of the top 2 cake layers. Remove the central sections, place these with the cake offcuts and set aside. You now have an intact first layer, with cut layers of cake above it forming sloping sides in the center of the stack. Use a small spatula to stick the 2 middle-layer side portions of cake to the first layer using some buttercream. Now stick each top side portion to the middle side portion beneath it with some buttercream.

2.

3.

3. Stack your fourth and fifth cake layers on a work surface. Take the template pieces labeled 'top'. Hold 1 against the center of one side of the top layer of the stack, so that the edge marked B on the template is flush with the top edge of the cake. Use toothpicks to hold the template in position. Position the duplicate template in the corresponding spot on the opposite side of the top layer. Using the diagonal lines at the sides of the templates to guide you, cut out the middle portion of the top cake layer with a long serrated knife. Remove the central section, place it in the bowl of cake offcuts and set aside. You now have an intact first layer, with a cut layer of cake above it forming sloping sides in the center of the small stack. Use a metal spatula to apply buttercream to the underside of each cut section to stick the side sections in position on the first layer.

4. Break the cake offcuts in the bowl into crumbs. Spoon 2 heaped tbsp of buttercream into the bowl and mix the frosting into the cake crumbs to form a paste. Divide the paste into 3 equal portions and place each portion in a separate bowl. Add a different shade of green coloring to each bowl to create 3 different shades of green.

5. Use 1 shade of green paste to fill the gap you created in the second layer of the 3-layer stack. Press the filling down firmly with the back of a spatula to level it out. Using a knife, carve away any of the green filling that may spill out of the front and back of the cake. Now use another shade of green paste to fill the gap in the top layer of the stack. Once again, press the filling down firmly with a spatula to level it out, and use a knife to carve away any spillage. Also, use the knife to level out the top of the green filling. Spread a thin layer of buttercream onto the white cake around the edges of the filled area.

5.

6. Fill the gap you created in the smaller stack with the final shade of green paste. Once again, flatten the filling with a spatula and carve away spillage. Now, carefully but quickly, invert the smaller stack and position it on the larger stack, lining up the 2 filled areas so that their combined shape forms that of a gem stone.

7. Crumb coat the entire cake (see page 20) with white buttercream. Refrigerate for 30 minutes to set. Prepare a pastry bag (see page 24), fitting it with a star piping tip (Wiltom 1M). Fill the pastry bag with the remaining buttercream. Pipe roses onto the cake (see page 25). Make a discreet mark in the bottom of your cake to mark the back, so you know which is the front of the cake. Refrigerate for 30 minutes.

6.

❧ Advanced Cakes ❧

Pirate Treasure Cake

This cake reveals a wonderful surprise and is perfect for a child's pirate-themed party, where everyone has a chance to grab some of the booty!

Preparation Time: 1 hour 45 minutes plus overnight drying, baking, and chilling | **Servings:** 15–20

3 lb 5 oz (1.5 kg) brown
  ready-to-use fondant
Confectioner's sugar, to dust
2 × 8-inch (20-cm) Chocolate
  Cakes (see page 14), leveled
1 × batch Dark Chocolate
  Ganache (see page 17)
3½ oz (100 g) gold chocolate
  coins
3½ oz (100 g) yellow
  gumpaste
¼ oz (10 g) white gumpaste

1. Cover a 9 inch (23 cm) by 12 inch (30 cm) cake board with brown fondant (see page 21). You'll need 1 yard (1 m) of brown ribbon. Wrap it around the edge of the board and secure it with double-sided tape. Leave the covered board out overnight to allow the fondant to dry.

2. Stack 1 cake on top of the other. Measure 5 inches (13 cm) along one side of the stack and carve away the remaining 3 inches (7 cm), leaving 2 stacked cake layers that are 8 inches (20 cm) in length and 5 inches (13 cm) in width. Discard the offcuts. Set aside 1 layer.

3. Slice the remaining layer in half horizontally to create 2 equal layers. Place a small amount of ganache onto the center of the prepared

cake board. Place 1 shallow layer on the board. Take the other shallow layer and measure a 2-inch (5-cm) thick border around the top, marking the inner corners of the border with toothpicks. Cut away the center using the toothpicks to guide you, cutting all the way through the cake to create a 2-inch (5-cm) thick border. Discard the center.

4. Now turn your attention to the layer on the board. Using an angled metal spatula, apply some ganache onto this layer, but only on the area that corresponds to the border you cut out in the previous step. Place the border on top, pressing down to stick the 2 layers together.

5. Place the chocolate coins inside the border, ensuring the recess is full but the coins do not extend beyond the height of the border.

6. Now turn your attention to the cake you set aside in step 2. Make 2 semi-circle templates—draw a circle with a 5-inch (13-cm) diameter and fold it in half, then cut along the fold line. Align each of your semi-circle templates to one width (a 5-inch/13-cm side) of the cake, using toothpicks to hold them in place. Using a long serrated knife, carve away the upper portion of the cake beyond the templates, creating the curved lid of your treasure chest. Using an angled metal spatula, apply some ganache to the top of the border of the cake on the presentation board and stick the lid to the border. Crumb coat the cake (see page 20) with ganache and refrigerate for 10 minutes to set.

7. Roll out the remaining brown fondant and cover the cake (see page 22). Press horizontal lines around the sides and on top of the cake using the blunt side of a paring knife to resemble wood panels.

8. Roll out strips of yellow gumpaste to a thickness of ⅛ inch (3 mm) and a width of 2 inches (5 cm). Use a dampened paintbrush stick these to the top, front, and back of the treasure chest to represent metal trim. Create a lock by forming a square out of yellow gumpaste and a keyhole shape with any remaining brown gumpaste (do this by making a small circle and triangle and placing these together). Use a dampened paintbrush to stick the lock to the front of the treasure chest and the keyhole to the lock. Hold them firmly in place for 1 minute to ensure they are stuck to the chest.

9. To finish, make a string of pearls by rolling the white gumpaste into small balls. Stick these to the board in a line.

Templates

These templates are here to help you make the some of the cake projects in this book. Photocopy or scan them and print them at 100 percent, then cut them out for use. The cake projects they correspond to explain how to use them.

Cloud Cake *Page 80*

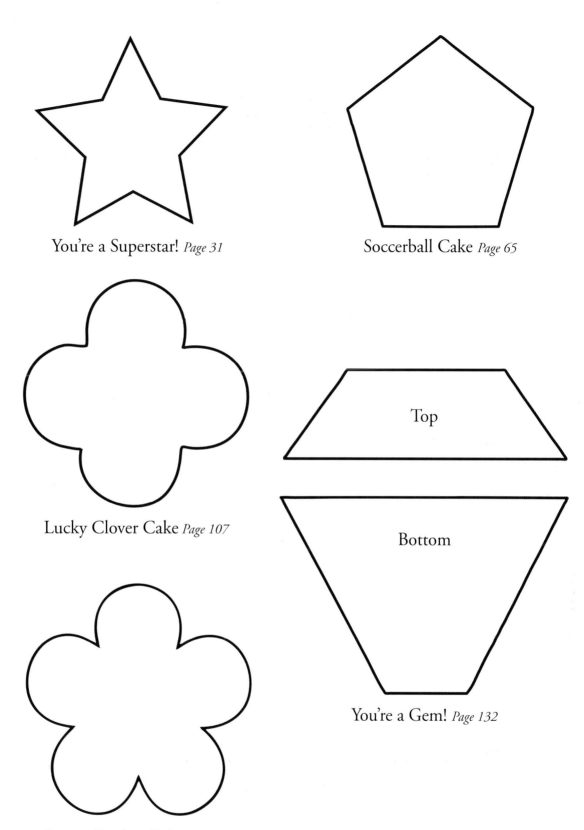

You're a Superstar! *Page 31*

Soccerball Cake *Page 65*

Lucky Clover Cake *Page 107*

Top

Bottom

You're a Gem! *Page 132*

Secret Garden Cake *Page 118*

Glossary

ALL-PURPOSE FLOUR
A wheat flour that can be used to make cakes.

BATTER
The mixture of dry and liquid ingredients that is poured into a cake pan and baked to make a cake.

BAKING POWDER
A product that is added to a cake recipe in order to allow it to rise.

BAKING SHEET
A stiff metal sheet on which to bake swiss rolls and other items, and on which cupcake pans and cake molds can be placed while baking in the oven. Baking sheets typically have edges.

BAKING SODA
A product that is added to a cake recipe in order to improve the effectiveness of other ingredients within the batter, such as the raising agents.

BLEND
To mix ingredients together to combine them, using hand-held tools such as a whisk, or in the bowl of a stand mixer.

BUTTERCREAM
A smooth frosting, used for filling and topping cakes, typically consisting of butter, confectioner's sugar and sometimes additional flavourings.

CAKE-LEVELING TOOL
A tool used to carve the tops off cakes in order to make the cakes leveled horizontally.

CAKE PAN
A pan that is specially made for baking cakes. Cake pans come in a variety of shapes and sizes.

COOKIE SHEET
A stiff metal sheet without edges on which to bake cookies and other items, and on which cupcake pans and cake molds can be placed while baking in the oven.

COCOA POWDER
Unsweetened cocoa powder is made using cacao beans and can be used in recipes to provide a chocolate flavour.

COOKIE CUTTER
A tool used to cut shapes out of pastry. In cake decorating, it can be used to cut shapes in fondant. These come in a variety of shapes and sizes.

CREAM (METHOD)
To mix the fats and sugars in a recipe by smoothing them together (typically with the back of a spoon or spatula) until they are combined.

CRUMB COAT
A layer of frosting or ganache used to hold the crumbs of the cake in place. This also works to prevent crumbs being seen in the final layer of frosting, ganache or fondant.

DOUGH
A mixture of ingredients made into a pliable substance.

DUST
To apply a light sprinkling, usually of flour or sugar.

DOUGH SCRAPER
A metal tool with a sharp edge, used to scrape dough off a surface. In cake decorating, this tool is used to give the sides of a frosted or ganached cake a smooth, professional-looking finish.

GEL FOOD COLORING
A gel-like substance used to add colors to fondant or cake batters. Gel food colors can be used in smaller amounts than liquid colorings, and tend to provide a stronger color.

FLAVORING
Liquids used in small amounts (usually by the teaspoon or less) to give cake batters and frostings specific flavors.

FROSTING
A thick filling or outer coating for cakes, with a buttery texture—usually buttercream.

FONDANT
A pliable sugar that is can be rolled out and used to cover cakes and make edible decorations for cakes.

FONDANT SMOOTHER
A tool used to give a professional, smooth finish to fondant-covered cakes.

GANACHE
A cream and chocolate mixture that is used to fill and cover cakes.

GUMPASTE
Much like fondant, gumpaste is used to make edible decorations for cakes. Gumpaste is firmer than fondant, and sets harder, so is better for making three-dimensional shapes.

LIQUID FOOD COLORING
A liquid used to add colors to cake batters and other foods.

SANDWICH PANS
Cake pans that are designed for making individual cake layers.

SANDWICH LAYERS
Thin layers of cake (normally around 2.5 cm/1 inch in thickness), often filled with different types of fillings.

SELF-RISING FLOUR
A flour product that can be used to make cakes. Cakes made with self-raising flour generally do not need additional raising agents, such as baking powder.

STACK/STACKING
To align cake layers of the same size in a vertical stack, often with an even layer of frosting between each cake layer in the stack.

STUCCO
A rough, textured effect used to decorate the outer layer of cakes with buttercream or ganache.

SUGAR
Confectioner's sugar
A powdered sugar product that is used for making frostings, dusting over finished cakes and on which to roll out fondant.

Superfine sugar
A fine sugar product often used in cake making.

Granulated sugar
A sugar with comparatively large grains.

Index

Acknowledgments

I would like to thank the following suppliers for generously providing some wonderful equipment and ingredients used for the photography for this book: Kenwood, for supplying a KMIX stand mixer, an essential piece of machinery in my kitchen; Secret Ingredients, for a mountain of sprinkles and toppings for the cakes and cupcakes; and Sugarcraft Boutique, for the fantastic equipment used to make projects within the book.

I have many people to thank, and it would be impossible to include absolutely everyone who has helped or influenced me in the making of this book, but I'll do my very best! First and foremost, I would like to thank my family – Christine, Daddy, André and Jenna – for the constant laughs and unconditional love, and my Nanny and Granddad, aunts and uncles, for their love, too. Thank you darling Davina, my best friend, my angel, for giving me much needed advice and love whenever I need it (big 'Mwah' to you!), and my gorgeous Sarah, my other best friend, for your unwavering support and guidance (and for slipping in entertaining Friends quotations wherever possible!). Thanks also to Krystal, my 'cake chum from another mom' – still here after decades of friendship. My gratitude goes to all my wonderful friends who have been there for me, sharing not only your ideas but also lending me your ears and shoulders when I need them most. Karen, my mentor, thank you for your positive presence and constant support. To my fellow professional baker Ceri, I am eternally grateful to you for putting this project into place, as well as for your valuable guidance and friendship.

Thank you Heather, my assistant, for your practical support, both in the preparation for and during the photo shoots. Thank you to Salima, my editor, who makes editing seem effortless! Thank you Tony, for bringing my cakes alive with your fantastic photography, and for your calming and encouraging manner throughout the photo shoots. And a huge thank you to the entire Quintet team, who have been gracious and helpful throughout, and who have offered me this opportunity to share my skills and ideas with you all.

About the author

Marsha Phipps is the creator and director of London-based cake design company Cakings. Largely self-taught, Marsha both bakes and designs bespoke cakes for her clients. These include handmade centrepieces for both corporate and personal celebrations. Her designs often feature detailed sugarcraft modeling, married with delicious cakes and tasty fillings. She also spends her time developing exciting flavors, experimenting with groundbreaking decorating techniques, and discussing the latest cake trends with her fans and customers via social media.

Her beautiful cakes and sugarcraft work can be seen here:
www.cakings.co.uk
https://www.facebook.com/CakingsCakes